Stevenson College Edinburgh.
Library

A22535

WITHDRAWN

KT-471-804

Top 25 locator map
(continues on inside
back cover)

CityPack
Paris

FIONA DUNLOP

If you have any comments
or suggestions for this guide
you can contact the editor at
Citypack@theAA.com

AA Publishing
Find out more about AA Publishing and the wide range
of travel publications and services the AA provides by
visiting our website at *www.theAA.com/bookshop*

About this Book

KEY TO SYMBOLS

🗺 Map reference to the accompanying fold-out map, and Top 25 locator map

✉ Address

☎ Telephone number

🕐 Opening/closing times

🍴 Restaurant or café on premises or nearby

Ⓜ Nearest Métro (underground) station

🚆 Nearest railway station

🚌 Nearest bus route

🚢 Nearest riverboat or ferry stop

♿ Facilities for visitors with disabilities

✋ Admission charges: Expensive (over €9), Moderate (€6–9) and Inexpensive (under €6)

↔ Other nearby places of interest

❓ Other practical information

▶ Indicates the page where you will find a fuller description

ℹ Tourist information

ORGANIZATION

This guide is divided into six sections:
- Planning Ahead and Getting There
- Living Paris—Paris Now, Paris Then, Time to Shop, Out and About, Walks, Paris by Night
- Paris's Top 25 Sights
- Paris's Best—best of the rest
- Where to detailed listings of restaurants, hotels, shops and nightlife
- Travel facts—packed with practical information

In addition, easy-to-read side panels provide extra facts and snippets, highlights of places to visit and invaluable practical advice.

The colours of the tabs on the page corners match the colours of the triangles aligned with the chapter names on the contents page opposite.

MAPS

The fold-out map in the wallet at the back of the book is a comprehensive street plan of Paris. The first (or only) map reference given for each attraction refers to this map. **The Top 25 locator maps** found on the inside front and back covers of the book itself are for quick reference. They show the Top 25 Sights, described on pages 26–50, which are clearly plotted by number (**1** – **25**, not page number) across the city. The second map reference given for the Top 25 Sights refers to this map.

Contents

WITHDRAWN
Stevenson College Edinburgh
Bankhead Ave EDIN EH11 4DE

Planning Ahead

WHEN TO GO

Spring is a popular time, with its lovely chestnut blossom. The city reaches peak tourist capacity in hot, sunny July. However, with the Parisian exodus to the countryside in August the city is emptier than usual, although there are fewer cultural activities. Autumn is busy with trade fairs, and rooms can be scarce and expensive.

TIME

Paris is one hour ahead of London, six hours ahead of New York and nine hours ahead of Los Angeles.

AVERAGE DAILY MAXIMUM TEMPERATURES

JAN	FEB	MAR	APR	MAY	JUN	JUL	AUG	SEP	OCT	NOV	DEC
45°F	45°F	50°F	61°F	63°F	73°F	77°F	79°F	70°F	61°F	54°F	46°F
7°C	7°C	10°C	16°C	17°C	23°C	25°C	26°C	21°C	16°C	12°C	8°C

Spring (April to May) takes time to get going in Paris and things don't usually warm up until mid-May.

Summer (June to August) can be glorious. Days are longest in June, with the most sunshine and a pleasant temperature. Hot and sunny in July, it is often hot, humid and stormy in August.

Autumn (September to November) has crisp days and clear skies.

Winter (December to March) is rarely below freezing, but it rains frequently, sometimes with hail, in January and March.

WHAT'S ON

January/February *Chinese New Year:* In Chinatown.

April/May *International Paris Fair:* Gastronomy, tourism, homes and gardens at Porte de Versailles; www.foiredeparis.fr

Paris marathon: Starts from the Champs Élysées; www.parismarathon.com

May *Labour Day* (1 May): Processions and symbolic lily-of-the-valley bouquets.

June *Festival Foire Saint-Germain:* Village traditions revived.

Fête de la Musique (21 Jun): Everything from classical to techno, both indoors and out.

Course des Garçons de Café (late Jun): Over 500 waiters and waitresses race through the streets, armed with tray, bottle and glasses.

July *Bastille Day* (14 Jul): The most important French festival celebrates the 1789 storming of the Bastille. Fireworks and street dances on the evening of the 13th and a parade on the 14th on the Champs Élysées.

July–August *Paris Quartier d'Été:* Outdoor concerts and street theatre.

September *Festival d'Automne à Paris* (mid-Sep to end Dec): Music, theatre and dance all over the city.

October *Foire Internationale d'Art Contemporain:* Paris's biggest modern art fair, at the Pavillon du Parc, Paris Expo, Porte de Versailles; www.fiac-online.com

November *Beaujolais Nouveau* (third Thu in Nov): Liberal amounts of wine are drunk when the first bottles hit Paris.

December *Paris International Boat Show:* At the Porte de Versailles; www.salonnautiqueparis.com

PARIS ONLINE

www.paris-ile-de-france.com or www.pidf.com
The site of the Paris Île de France regional tourist authority, with a huge quantity and variety of information on Paris and the surrounding region —entertainment and events, shopping, sport, leisure, kids' Paris, accommodation and public transport.

www.paris-touristoffice.com
The Paris Tourist Office online, with listings and practical information, sightseeing and links to other useful sites covering every aspect of leisure in the city. There is a selection of the week's events and you can even find out the air quality in the city.

www.parisfranceguide.com
This site, aimed at English-speakers, is about getting orientated in Paris and finding what you are looking for—a job and an apartment, a hotel or events information.

www.parisvoice.com
Click here and you'll feel like you're already in the city. Intended for English-speaking Parisians, it gives an insider's view of the city, with features, events information, restaurant reviews, classified ads, a Q & A column (dealing with some very serious issues), a Where to Kiss in Paris guide and more.

www.paris.fr
The official site of Paris' mayor and city council has information on museums, theatres, parks and sport, as well as a virtual tour of the Hôtel de Ville. There is also a wealth of civic news aimed at Paris residents.

www.parissi.com
All the Paris disco, dance and clubland news (in French). With the latest programmes from the city's main nightclubs and late-night bars, this is *the* place for party animals and clubbers to plan sleepless Paris visits. Links to some other wacky sights as well.

PRIME TRAVEL SITES

www.ratp.fr
The official site of RATP, the Paris bus and Métro network, is packed with useful information. The English section has a helpful route planner. In the French section click on Visiter Paris for detailed advice on using public transport, as well as walks, events and museums.

www.parisdigest.com
Independent city guide showing you around the city and providing a huge quantity of fascinating practical information. A good range of hotel, restaurant and shopping guides.

www.paris.worldweb.com
Lots of information on the different neighbourhoods of Paris. Travel facts, museum guide, hotels and restaurants. Links to other regions of France listing tours, activities and travel details.

www.fodors.com
A complete travel-planning site. You can research prices and weather; book air tickets, cars and rooms; ask questions (and get answers) from fellow travellers; and find links to other sites.

Getting There

VISAS AND TRAVEL INSURANCE

Visas are not required for EU, US or Canadian nationals, but you will need a valid passport. EU citizens receive reduced-cost medical treatment with form E111, but full insurance is still strongly advised and is essential for all other travellers.

MONEY

The euro is the official currency of France. Bank notes in denominations of 5, 10, 20, 50, 100, 200 and 500 euros and coins in denominations of 1, 2, 5, 10, 20 and 50 cents and 1 and 2 euros were introduced on 1 January 2002.

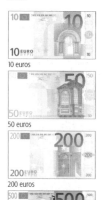

10 euros

50 euros

200 euros

500 euros

ARRIVING

Most international flights arrive at Roissy Charles de Gaulle airport, with some international and French domestic flights arriving at Orly airport. Paris has good rail connections, including the Eurostar train direct from London.

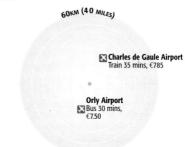

60KM (40 MILES)

⊠ **Charles de Gaule Airport**
Train 35 mins, €785

Orly Airport
⊠ Bus 30 mins,
€7.50

FROM ROISSY CHARLES DE GAULLE

Roissy (☎ 01 48 62 22 80; www.adp.fr) is 23km (14 miles) northeast of central Paris. There are three terminals. Air France currently operates out of Terminal 2. You can get to the city in three ways. By bus: Air France (www.cars-airfrance.com) operates a bus service between the airport and Montparnasse and Gare de Lyon, every 30 minutes 7am–9.30pm (€11.50), and to the Arc de Triomphe every 15 minutes, 5.45am–11pm (€10). Alternatively take the 50-minute trip on Roissybus that runs every 15 minutes from Terminals 1, 2 and 3 to Opéra from 5.45am –11pm (€8.20). By train: A surburban train network RER (Réseau Express Régional) takes around 35 minutes into central Paris (€7.85). Trains leave every 15 minutes. By taxi: A taxi costs around €50 and takes between 30 minutes and 1 hour, depending on traffic (confirm price first).

FROM ORLY

Orly (☎ 01 49 75 15 15; www.adp.fr), the older and smaller of Paris's two main international airports, is 14km (8.5 miles) south of central Paris with no direct public transport links. By bus: Air

France provides shuttle buses to Les Invalides and Gare Montparnasse every 15 minutes 5.45am–11pm (€7.50). The trip takes about 30 minutes. By train: The Orlyval train, which operates Mon–Sun 6am–11pm will take you two stops to Antony where you can change for line B of the main Paris RER rail system (€8.85). From here it's around 30 minutes to central Paris. By taxi: A taxi costs around €35 and takes 15–30 minutes. Confirm the price first.

FROM EUROSTAR

The Eurostar (☎ 08705 186 186 from the UK; www.eurostar.com) takes you right into the heart of Paris to the Gare du Nord. From here there are good Métro and RER connections, or you can take a taxi.

GETTING AROUND

The best way to travel around Paris is by Métro or RER, two separate but linked systems. The RER is the suburban line, which passes through the heart of the city. The Métro is the city's underground system, with 14 lines and over 300 stations. Both are inexpensive and efficient, and free maps of all the routes are available at station ticket windows. Everywhere is within easy walking distance of a Métro or RER station. Both systems function the same way and the tickets are interchangeable. It is cheaper to buy a *carnet* of 10 tickets than to buy each ticket separately. For more information ► 91.

Travelling by batobus—a river shuttle boat—is fun. It operates May–end Sep daily 10–9; Mar–end Apr, Oct 10–7; Nov–end Dec 10.30–4.30 stopping at the Eiffel Tower, Musée d'Orsay, Saint-Germain-des-Prés, Notre-Dame, Jardin des Plantes, The Hôtel de Ville, the Louvre and Champs Élysées. You can join at any point.

Taxis can be hailed in the street if the roof sign is illuminated, or can be found at most main attractions in taxi ranks. Sunday and night rates (7pm–7am) rise considerably and extra charges are made at stations for luggage. Taxi drivers expect tips of 10 per cent.

HANDY HINT

If you plan to visit many sights, get a *Carte Musées et Monuments* that offers free access to 60 attractions in Paris and the Île de France. Cards are valid for 1, 3 or 5 days and can be readily bought at museums, metro stations and FNAC desks.

VISITORS WITH DISABILITIES

Careful planning is advisable for any visitor with disabilities travelling to Paris, which has a poor record on access and amenities. On the Métro, only the Meteor line (no. 14) has easy access for people with disabilities. Buses are similarly poorly equipped. RATP's Les Compagnons du Voyage (☎ 01 53 11 11 12) provides companions for visitors with disabilities (if not in a wheelchair), but for a fee. However, taxis are obliged to assist wheelchair travellers in every way.

The website of the Paris Tourist Office (www.paris-touristoffice.com) has useful information for visitors with disabilities, including a list of accessible sights. You can also try www.holidaycare.org

STEVENSON COLLEGE
LIBRARY

ACC. No.	A 22535	
CLASS/LOC	SRC 914.436 DUN	
CAT 286051AW	PROC	

Living
Paris

Paris Now

Above: *Café on the boulevard Saint-Germain*
Right: *Fountains play on the place de la Concorde*

DECLINING NUMBERS

• In 1851, Paris represented 3 per cent of the total population of France. By 1954, 15 per cent of the nation's population lived here. But in 2001, the figure stood again at just 4 per cent—almost the same as 150 years ago—as the population continued to move into the suburbs, which are in the île de France rather than part of Paris.

Paris is more than a city, more than a place. It is an idea, a grand vision, the very symbol of civilization, culture, refinement, romance, flair, energy and *savoir faire*. Not just the capital of France, it feels more like the capital city of the whole of Europe. No one feels that more than Parisians themselves.

There's something stirring in the air, in the light, in the muted hues. As soon as you walk out of the Gare du Nord you feel it. Brave the hurtling Gallic traffic and cross the cobbled roadway to the brasseries across the road. An espresso, an aperitif or a meal makes the perfect start to a few days under the spell of the French capital.

Of course, it *is* just a city, with crazy drivers, crowded streets, puzzling public transport and risky neighbourhoods. Yet an instrinsic conservatism and good taste gives the city incomparable appeal. There are few high-rises.

JACQUES CHIRAC

• For over 18 years Jacques Chirac, the ebullient mayor of Paris and leader of the Gaullist party (RPR, now UMP), surveyed the city from his palatial working residence overlooking the Seine, the Hôtel de Ville, and relaxed by reading Chinese poetry in French. He transformed the city's infrastructure and repeatedly clashed with the ruling Socialists until in May 1995, after two previously unsuccessful attempts, he was finally elected president of France. He was re-elected in 2002, helped by a protest vote against his far-right opponent, Jean-Marie Le Pen.

Above: *The airy glass pyramid at the Louvre, designed by I. M. Pei, forms the main entrance to the museum*

11

Above: *Ancient meets modern—stone statue outside the beautiful church of Saint-Eustache*
Above right: *Interior of the popular Café Beaubourg*

POPULAR PARIS

• Only 2.1 million people live within the city boundary of Paris today. Of these, only 20 per cent live in the centre. But 11 million live in the suburbs, and there are around 20 million foreign visitors each year, making Paris the world's most popular city. The Louvre alone has over 6 million visitors annually.

Long, straight avenues converging on the hub are all lined with buildings in the same florid century-old architectural style. In the heart of the city itself, majestic terraces and squares of beautifully restored gilded mansions set a dignified tone. Wherever some new structure has been erected, it is not just a building, but great art, a flight of fancy, a grand project, a monument, a masterpiece.

Above all, the people make Paris. Call it class, or panache. Rich or poor, Parisians walk, dress and talk with razor-edge precision and style. Appearance matters—whatever the occasion. You won't see many in tracksuits, leggings or lycra, except at the gym.

Hop from Montmartre to Montparnasse, from the Arc de Triomphe to place de la Bastille, and you've covered central Paris. It's small enough to be explored on foot, and this is the best way to absorb its complex flavour and atmosphere. Let the city lead you, and do not believe the old cliché that Parisians are unfriendly—though that may be true of harassed, overworked waiters and shopkeepers. Wander in the winding backstreets

Above: *Luxembourg Gardens*

and Paris unfolds as a collection of villages, each with its little squares and neighbourhood shops.

For just as France is a nation of *régions*, so Paris is a city of *quartiers*. Its 20 administrative *arrondissements* each have their own character, making the city a veritable mosaic.

Stroll from one to the next and you may move from Africa to Asia, the Caribbean into the Arab world. The Marais, in the 4th, includes the city's oldest Jewish quarter, now gentrified by a new

PARIS'S CANALS

● Cruising the city's canals offers a more idiosyncratic view of Paris than the usual Seine trip. The revamped Arsenal dock at the Bastille (1806) is the kick-off for an underground vaulted passage that re-emerges at the Canal Saint-Martin. Chestnut trees, swing-bridges, locks, the Hôtel du Nord and modern apartment blocks all make for a great trip.

SOCIALISTS RETURN

● Despite the city's revolutionary reputation, and the election of Socialists at national level, Paris remained firmly under right wing control for almost the whole of the 20th century. The mayoral elections of 25 March 2001 produced a bombshell. For the first time since the Paris Commune, the working class revolt of 1871, the capital of France was to be ruled by the Left. On taking office Paris' new Socialist mayor, Bertrand Delanoe, declared—'For the first time since 1909, the forces for progress hold the majority. Paris is still the capital of the movement, a focus for audacity and generosity. With the struggle of Etienne Marcel and the Commune, with the Declaration of the Rights of Man and the Liberation of the city, Paris has tirelessly told a tale of a city that will neither conform nor submit.'

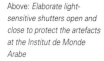

Above: *Elaborate light-sensitive shutters open and close to protect the artefacts at the Institut de Monde Arabe*

ON TOP OF THE WORLD

• 'Paris is complete, Paris is the ceiling of humanity. Whoever sees Paris thinks he sees the basis of all history. Paris is synonymous with the cosmos—it has no limits. It does more than make the law, it makes fashion. It is more than great, it is immense'— Victor Hugo, *Les Misérables*.

generation of entrepreneurs. Across the river, Saint-Germain-des-Prés is the smart end of the Left Bank, haunt of Paris society's most successful, intellectual and creative élite. A few streets away, you can absorb the heady student culture of the Quartier Latin. *Grands Projets,* initiated under President Mitterrand, are completely changing the face of some districts—riverside Bercy, for example, east of the city's core, has been reborn.

Behind the scenes long standing corruption is being flushed out. At the same time public works are underway. As the 21st century approached, the French economy grew at a phenomenal rate; and Paris benefited. Big-name Paris-based companies have extended their international reach, sometimes acquiring significant American and Japanese competitors. The internet and new media have been grasped with enthusiasm and flair, and there is even a willingness to use the once scorned English

language. International sporting triumphs also gave a fillip to the city's, and the nation's, sense of pride. The mood is up-beat, forward-looking and optimistic.

Above: *A view underneath La Grande Arche in La Defense area*
Left: *It's best to take the Métro or walk when sightseeing in Paris*

Yet Paris and Parisians re-main at heart thoroughly traditionalist. The city is still the world's greatest gastronomic capital. True, innovation is no longer frowned upon in the kitchen, and even exotic foreign food makes an appearance. But when Paris sits down to dine, classic French dishes are on the menu, washed down with French wines.

Let yourself succumb to the city's charms: See the great art museums and the famous sights, take a *bateau mouche* down the Seine, walk on the quaysides of the Cité, people-watch from a café, admire the view from the Sacré Cœur, enjoy a good dinner, go to a show. The classic formula will beguile you—as it does the Parisians themselves.

PARIS PLAGE

● Many Parisians desert the city in the height of summer, but for those who don't, there is a new way to keep cool. 'Paris Plage' made its first appearance in 2002, when imported sand, palm trees and deck chairs turned part of the Right Bank into a beach for a month. It looks set to become a regular feature in the years to come.

15

Paris Then

Above: *The Hundred Years War—Battle of Sluis, 1340*

BEFORE 1000

Celtic tribe of Parisii settles on Île de la Cité around 200BC.

By AD100 the Roman city of Lutetia, later Paris, is growing fast.

In 451 Saint Geneviève saves Paris from the threat of Attila the Hun.

REIGN OF TERROR

From 1793–94 the Reign of Terror had seized France, masterminded by the ruthless, power-crazed Jacobin leaders Robespierre and Danton. The king, Louis XVI, was convicted of treason and guillotined in January 1793, followed in October by his queen, Marie-Antoinette. By mid-1794 some 17,000 people had been beheaded in France.

1163 The rebuilding of Notre Dame starts.

1337– 1453 Hundred Years War between France and England.

1431 Henry VI of England crowned king of France in Notre Dame.

1437 Charles VII regains control of Paris.

1572 St. Bartholomew Massacre ignites Wars of Religion.

1682 Louis XIV and the court move to Versailles.

1700s Development of Faubourg Saint-Germain.

1789 Storming of the Bastille.

1792 Monarchy abolished; proclamation of the Republic.

1804 Napoleon crowned emperor.

1830 Bourbons overthrown; Louis-Philippe crowned.

1848 Revolution topples Louis-Philippe; Second Republic headed by Napoleon III, later crowned emporer.

1852–70 Baron Haussmann, employs architects to transform Paris.

1870–71	Paris besieged by Prussians, civil uprising of the Commune, Republic restored.
1889	Eiffel Tower is completed.
1900	First Métro line opens.
1914–18	Paris bombarded by German cannon, Big Bertha.
1940	Nazis occupy Paris, followed by Liberation in 1944.
1958	De Gaulle heads Fifth Republic.
1977	Jacques Chirac elected mayor (he becomes president in 1995). Centre Georges Pompidou opens.
1981	Election of President Mitterrand. He initiates his *Grands Projets*—a scheme of new building projects.
1998	France wins football (soccer) World Cup as host nation.
1999	December storms hit Paris; Versailles loses over 10,000 trees.
2002	Euro notes and coins introduced.
2004	Paris celebrates the centenary of the Entente Cordiale between the United Kingdom and France.

From second left:
St. Bartholomew's Day Massacre, 1572; Paris Commune uprising, 1871; construction of the Eiffel Tower, 1888; General de Gaulle leads the crowds on Liberation Day, 25 August 1944

THE SEINE

The city's history has been inextricably linked with the Seine since its earliest origins as a Gaulish village on the Île de la Cité, an islet in the river.

The river represents the very lifeblood of Paris, flowing through its heart, animating the city, defining the capital geographically and reflecting its history in its many fine buildings.

After centuries of pollution —when the river was used as a sewer—the Seine has been cleaned and its water is less polluted than it has been for years.

17

Time to Shop

Below: *Antique market close to place de la Bastille*
Below right: *Chic shopping— Hermès in the fashionable rue du Faubourg Saint-Honoré*

Narrow rue du Faubourg Saint-Honoré has the classiest shopping in the city, with Gucci, Versace, Hermès and Karl Lagerfeld, and several other top fashion names almost next door to each other. Prices are high but it certainly deserves a lingering window-shop if nothing

WHAT'S WHAT

With so much to see and so many windows to look in, go prepared. *Boulangeries* sell the famous French *baguettes*, and much more besides; try the *ficelle*, a thinner, finer loaf; a *fluiot*—rye bread with walnuts, hazelnuts and raisins. And, of course there are the croissants, *ordinaire* or *au beurre* (with butter). *Pâtisseries* sell a range of mouth-watering pastries and tarts. *Charcuteries* sell far more than cold meats—snails, cheese, truffles, wine and caviar to name but a few. *Parfumeries* can be solely devoted to French perfume, but some may sell cosmetics and soaps too. *Bouquinistes* (dealers in old books) sell first editions and old prints, posters and postcards.

else. It ends at rue Royale and place de la Madeleine, ringed by the greatest of Parisian food shops. There are many specialists in truffles, handmade chocolates, caviar and the queen of all food halls, Fauchon, stacked high with gastronomic luxuries, is here.

Visitors from all over the country crowd into this area in search of the latest designer fashions and the fine foods. It's only a few minutes to boulevard Haussman and the city's two stylish principal belle epoque department stores, Galeries Lafayette and Printemps; complete with English-speaking hostesses. Try to catch the free Lafayette fashion shows, which are an experience in themselves.

Near the Pompidou Centre is the old Halles marketplace, now a popular indoor shopping area. In the Sentier and Opéra districts just north, explore delightful covered alleys and shop-lined 19th-century *galeries*, which are an excellent place to linger if the weather is poor.

Nip across the Seine, by Métro or on foot, to Saint-Germain-des-Prés. The grown-up part of the Left Bank is the place for antiquarian bookshops, antique dealers, art galleries and, further south, the city's oldest department store, Le Bon Marché, at 22 rue des Sèvres.

Below left: Interior of the Galeries Lafayette store
Below: Galerie Vivienne, built in 1823, continues to offer stylish shopping

In Paris look for French flair and quality, not bargains. Think not only fashion, lingerie and perfume, but high-quality cookware such as Le Creuset, superb knives by Sabatier, wonderful copper pans for making sauces and kitchen gadgets such as perfect openers for champagne bottles and whisks that really work. Think also of stylish children's and baby clothes, plus of course prepared goods—ready to buy *coq au vin*—pâtes and unusual wines. If you can read French, browse the gastronomy section in any bookshop for excellent guides to French regional cuisine.

If it's souvenirs of Paris you want you will find no shortage of cheap replicas of the Eiffel Tower, especially from sellers beneath the tower. You'll find better versions as paperweights in the specialist shops. Or bring home a Peugeot peppermill, a fine piece of kitchen engineering, or visit the galleries such as the Louvre, Musée d'Orsay and Musée Marmottan for postcards of the Mona Lisa, prints by Monet and posters of the Folies Bergères by Henri de Toulouse-Lautrec.

GOURMET PICNICS

There isn't a word for delicatessen in French. A *charcuterie* is a pork butcher and a *traiteur* a caterer, or a shop selling ready-cooked dishes. In practice, the two are closely related, and are often combined into one. Inside, glass cabinets or counters display dozens of exquisite freshly prepared salads, grated carrots, paper-thin slices of cucumber, aubergines (egg plant), mushrooms, and garlic, beans-and-pork stew, a gourmet mix of cooked meats, meat pies and spicy sausages.

Out and About

Above: *The glorious ceiling of the upper chapel at Sainte-Chapelle*

Above right: *Parisians love to escape the hectic city and find refuge in its many green spaces*

INFORMATION

VERSAILLES

✉ Château de Versailles
☎ 01 30 83 78 00
🕐 State apartments
Apr–end Oct Tue–Sun
9–6.30; Nov–end Mar
9–5.30. Grand and Petit
Trianon daily noon–5.30
(until 6.30 in summer).
Park daily 7am–sunset (8
in winter). Fountains
Apr–end Sep Sat–Sun
10.30–noon, 3.30–5
🍴 Cafés, restaurants
🚆 RER C Versailles Rive
Gauche
♿ Few (part of State
apartments)
💰 Chateau moderate,
free for visitors with
disabilities; park free
🎫 Guided Tours

ITINERARIES
LATIN QUARTER

Start the day with a climb up the tower of Notre Dame (➤ 45) for a bird's eye view over the city. Walk by the river to the Sainte Chapelle (➤ 41). Cross the river to boulevard Saint-Michel and walk up to the Musée de Cluny (➤ 40). Continue up boulevard Saint-Michel to the Jardin du Luxembourg (➤ 39). Have lunch in a café near the Panthéon. Walk to Église Saint-Étienne-du-Mont (➤ 54). Explore the winding streets to the rue Monge. Look at the Roman Arènes de Lutèce (➤ 61). Walk south towards the Mosquée (➤ 54) and indulge in a mint tea. Visit the Jardin des Plantes botanical garden and Muséum National d'Histoire Naturelle (➤ 53).

GREEN PARIS

Start the day out in the 16th *arrondissement* at the Musée Marmottan (➤ 26), devoted to the paintings of Monet, then take the Métro to Franklin D. Roosevelt. Walk down the paths of the Champs Élysées (➤ 29) to place de la Concorde (➤ 32). Cross over and walk through the Tuileries (➤ 58), stopping for a drink at a kiosk or along the terrasse du Bord de l'Eau for lovely views of the Left Bank. Have lunch at the Café Marly (➤ 55) or in the Louvre's subterranean labyrinth. Visit a section of the Louvre's immense collection (➤ 37), then recover in the gardens of the Palais Royal (➤ 61). Take bus No. 67 from the rue du Louvre to Pigalle, where you can catch the Montmartrobus to the top of Montmartre hill. The views from Sacré Cœur (➤ 35) are superb.

EXCURSIONS
CHÂTEAU AND PARK OF VERSAILLES
Versailles is the ultimate symbol of French grandeur, and the backdrop to the death of the monarchy. In 1661, when Louis XIV announced his intention of moving his court to this deserted swamp, it was to create a royal residence, seat of government and home to French nobility. Building continued until his death in 1715, by which time the 100-ha (247-acre) park had been tamed to perfection by landscape garden designer André Le Nôtre. Hundreds of statues, follies and fountains, and the royal retreats of the Grand and Petit Trianon relieve the formal symmetry, while rowing boats, bicycles and a minitrain now offer a diversion from history. Inside the château, visit the Grands Appartements (State apartments), which include the staggeringly ornate Hall of Mirrors. The Petits Apartements display France's most priceless examples of 18th-century decoration and may be visited by guided tour only.

GIVERNY
This small Normandy village is famous for one reason—Claude Monet. The painter lived here from 1883 until his death in 1926, inspiring a local artists' colony and producing some of Impressionism's most famous and startling canvases. His carefully tended garden with its Japanese-style lily pond gradually became his sole inspiration, and was as important to him as his painting. Only reproductions of his works are displayed, but the colourfully painted house, his personal collection of Japanese prints and the beautiful garden together offer a wonderful day out. May and June, when the borders are a riot of colour, is the best time for the flowers.

Above left: *The mighty Château de Versailles viewed from the south parterre*
Middle: *the staggeringly ornate Hall of Mirrors at Versailles*
Above: *Claude Monet's Japanese-style lily pond in the garden at Giverny*

INFORMATION

GIVERNY
✉ Fondation Claude Monet, rue Claude Monet, 27620 Giverny
☎ 02 32 51 28 21
🕐 Apr–end Oct Tue–Sun 9.30–6
🍴 Restaurant
🚆 SNR Gare St-Lazare to Vernon, then bus, taxi, hire a bike or walk (5km/3 miles)
♿ Good
💷 Inexpensive

Stevenson College Edinburgh
Bankhead Ave EDIN EH11 4DE

Walks

INFORMATION

Distance 3km (2 miles)
Time 2 hours
Start point ★ Plateau Beaubourg
⊞ N6
◎ Rambuteau, Hôtel de Ville
End point place des Vosges
⊞ Q7
🍴 Café Beaubourg, rue Saint-Merri (► 55); Ma Bourgogne, place des Vosges (► 71)

LE MARAIS TO THE PLACE DES VOSGES

After breakfast at the Café Beaubourg walk behind the Centre Georges Pompidou and turn right onto the rue Rambuteau, a colourful food-shopping street. Turn left up the rue des Archives, with the magnificent turreted Porte Clisson (1375) rising from the Hôtel de Soubise (1709) on your right. Continue past a monumental fountain (1624) on your left and the 1650 Hôtel Guénégaud, which houses the Musée de la Chasse, diagonally opposite. Keep walking straight onto the rue de Bretagne, turn right, enter the picturesque food and flower market of Les Enfants Rouges, then exit onto the rue Charlot.

Walk south past the Cathédrale Sainte-Croix-de-Paris to the rue des Quatre-Fils. Turn left and continue to the rue Vieille-du-Temple. Circle round the garden of the Hôtel Salé, now home to the Musée Picasso, then continue to rue du Parc-Royal, where a small garden is overlooked by a row of restored 17th-century mansions. Pausing at the courtyard of the Hôtel de Chatillon at 13 rue Payenne, continue to rue de Sévigné. Admire the mansions of the Musée Carnavalet, then continue across to the picturesque place du Marché Sainte-Catherine. Turn left into rue Saint-Antoine and left again to the place des Vosges.

0 _____ 1 km

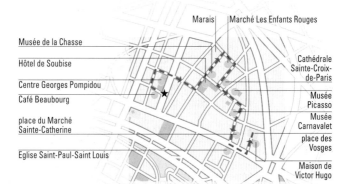

Musée de la Chasse
Hôtel de Soubise
Centre Georges Pompidou
Café Beaubourg
place du Marché Sainte-Catherine
Eglise Saint-Paul-Saint Louis

Marais | Marché Les Enfants Rouges
Cathédrale Sainte-Croix-de-Paris
Musée Picasso
Musée Carnavalet
place des Vosges
Maison de Victor Hugo

Place Des Vosges to the Latin Quarter

Walk through a passageway at No. 9 place des Vosges to the courtyard of the Hôtel de Sully.

Exit on to the rue Saint-Antoine, turn right and cross to rue Saint-Paul, lined with antique shops. Further down on the right enter the Village Saint-Paul (11–7, Thu–Mon), a discreetly situated bric-a-brac market, then emerge on the other side into the rue des Jardins Saint-Paul.

Here you see the largest remaining section of Philippe-Auguste's city wall.

Turn left, then right along the rue de l'Ave Maria to reach the Hôtel de Sens, an exceptional example of 15th-century Gothic architecture.

Look at the courtyard and the small formal garden behind the mansion. From here cross the Pont Marie to the Île Saint-Louis, turn right and walk along the quai de Bourbon and the quai d'Orléans, admiring the 17th-century mansions and the view of Notre Dame across the Pont Saint-Louis.

Cross the Pont de la Tournelle to the Left Bank and end your day in the web of the Latin Quarter across the Seine.

Distance 2km (1 mile)
Time 1–2 hours
Start point ★ place des Vosges
Q7
Bastille, Chemin Vert, St-Paul
End point Latin Quarter, around boulevard Saint-Michel, rue Saint-Jacques
L8

0   1 km

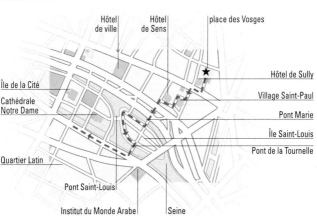

Paris by Night

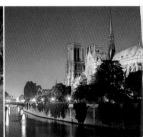

Paris's buildings look stunning illuminated at night

AN EVENING STROLL

Start at Châtelet and walk towards the Louvre along the embankment opposite the illuminated Conciergerie, the Monnaie (Mint) and the Institut de France. At the Louvre make a detour into the Cour Carrée, magnificently lit and often deserted at night. Return to the river, cross the lively Pont des Arts, then walk back along the opposite bank, this time with views north of the stately Samaritaine and the Palais de Justice on the Île de la Cité. Continue towards Saint-Michel, then cross over to Notre Dame and make your way around the north side of the island, which offers views of the Île Saint-Louis, the Hôtel de Ville and the Gothic Tour Saint-Jacques towering over the place du Châtelet.

The heart of Paris has a special beauty at night, and an electric atmosphere. Boulevards, great monuments and historic buildings are dazzlingly illuminated. The Champs-Elysées, place de la Concorde and the Louvre make a magnificent spectacle of lights against the night sky. The soaring Eiffel Tower, shining like gold, and the silvery white of the Sacré Cœur Basilica are majestic landmarks. The main streets are busy; many bars and even some restaurants staying open until well after midnight.

There's a sense of excitement, anticipation and enjoyment. In addition to the glamorous cabarets, there are the world-class ballet, concert and opera venues, scores of nightclubs, discos, café-theatres and atmospheric bars with live music. Travelling in the city at night is simple, and in the central areas can be enjoyable. Although the Métro is closed from 12.30am to 5.45am, there are many taxis at night, as well as the Noctambus services that radiate from Châtelet to all districts.

A boat trip along the Seine between the illuminated buildings adds an extra magic—*bateaux mouches* run every evening until 11pm (9pm in winter), and also offer a 4-course dinner cruise option. For experienced in-line skaters a high-speed three-hour skating tour of Paris takes place every Friday at 10pm (www.pari-roller.com for details). Where *not* to be at night, unless you are looking for the city's sleaziest clubs and revues, are the boulevard de Clichy and place Pigalle, at the foot of Montmartre.

PARIS's
top 25 sights

The sights are shown on the maps on the inside front cover and inside back cover, numbered **1** – **25** across the city

Musée Marmottan

INFORMATION

www.marmottan.com

- ⊕ Off map at A6; Locator map off A3
- ✉ 2 rue Louis-Boilly 75016
- ☎ 01 44 96 50 33
- ⏰ Tue–Sun 10–6 (last admission 5.30)
- Ⓜ La Muette
- 🚌 32
- 🚆 RER Line C Boulainvilliers
- 💶 Moderate
- 🔁 Bois de Boulogne (➤ 58)

The Marmottan Museum is located in the residential 16th *arrondissement*, where a mesmerizing collection of Monet paintings makes for a colourful escape from the urban aspects of the Parisian landscape.

Rich donations This often overlooked treasure of Parisian culture offers an eclectic collection built up over the years from the original donation of Renaissance and First Empire paintings and furniture given to the nation by the art historian Paul Marmottan in 1932. His discreetly elegant 19th-century mansion, furnished with Renaissance tapestries and sculptures and Napoleonic furniture, was later given an extra boost by the stunning Wildenstein collection of 230 illustrated manuscripts from the 13th to the 16th centuries, as well as an exceptional donation from Michel Monet of works by his father Claude Monet, the Impressionist painter. Other generous donations include works by Monet's contemporaries Gauguin, Renoir, Pissarro, Sisley, Berthe Morisot and Gustave Caillebotte, thus adding to the Impressionist focus, but it is above all Monet's luminous canvases of dappled irises, wisteria and water-lilies, dating from his last years at Giverny, that are memorable.

Shame It happens even to the best of museums, but when nine major paintings were stolen from the Marmottan in 1985 it caused acute embarrassment, not least because the booty included Monet's seminal work, *Impression—soleil levant,* that gave the art movement its name. Five years later, after a police operation on a worldwide scale, the plundered paintings were discovered in Corsica and displayed once again, needless to say under greatly increased security.

Palais de Chaillot

With its majestic wings curving towards the Eiffel Tower across the Seine, and its monumental presence, the Palais de Chaillot impresses. But it also has a human aspect: skaters, mime artists and Sunday promenaders.

Attractions The 1937 Exposition Universelle instigated the Palais de Chaillot's columns, punctuated with bronze statues that overlook terraces and fountains. This spectacular art-deco wrapping contains two museums (three if the Salon de Musique is considered a museum), and the Théâtre de Chaillot. The west wing houses the Musée de la Marine, catering to maritime and naval interests, and the Musée de l'Homme devoted to anthropology, currently being restructured. A large part of its ethnological collections will be transferred to the new Musée du quai Branly (► 53) due to open in 2006; meanwhile, the museum houses three thematic exhibitions dedicated to aspects of mankind.

Fire The building's east wing was damaged by fire in 1997 and its two museums are now closed. The Musée du Cinéma will be relocated in the former American Center (51 rue de Bercy), converted into a complex entirely dedicated to the cinema. The Musée

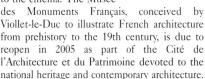

An exhibit in the maritime museum

des Monuments Français, conceived by Viollet-le-Duc to illustrate French architecture from prehistory to the 19th century, is due to reopen in 2005 as part of the Cité de l'Architecture et du Patrimoine devoted to the national heritage and contemporary architecture.

HIGHLIGHTS

- View of the Eiffel Tower
- Napoleon's imperial barge
- *Ports de France,* Vernet
- *Le Valmy*
- Contemporary French navy
- *Le Louis XV*, model of a 17th-century 3-decked ship
- Lucy's skeleton

INFORMATION

- A5–A6; Locator map A2
- place du Trocadéro 75116
- Marine 01 53 65 69 69; www.musee-marine.fr Homme 01 44 05 72 72; www.mnhn.fr
- Marine Wed–Mon 10–6; Homme Wed–Fri, Mon 9.45–5.15, Sat–Sun 10–6.30
- Café-restaurant place du Trocadéro
- Trocadéro
- 22, 30, 32, 63
- Few
- Marine moderate; Homme moderate
- Musée d'Art Moderne de la Ville de Paris (► 52)
- Guided tours of both museums–information on request

Tour Eiffel

HIGHLIGHTS

- Panoramic views
- Bust of Gustave Eiffel

DID YOU KNOW?

- Weight: over 10,000 tonnes
- Made of 18,000 iron sections
- Height: 324m (1,050ft)
- Top platform at 276m (905ft)
- 1,665 steps to the top
- 60 tonnes of paint needed to repaint it
- 370 suicides

INFORMATION

www.tour-eiffel.fr
- B7; Locator map A3
- Champ de Mars 75007
- 01 44 11 23 23
- Sep–mid-Jun 9am–midnight (stairs 9.30–6.30); mid-Jun–end Aug daily 9.30am–11pm; last admission 1 hour before closing
- Altitude 95 (1st floor 01 45 55 20 04); Jules Verne (2nd floor 01 45 55 61 44)
- Bir-Hakeim, Trocadéro
- 42, 69, 82, 87
- RER Line C, Tour Eiffel
- Very good (to 2nd floor)
- Expensive; stairs inexpensive
- Les Invalides (➤ 30)

The Eiffel Tower could be a cliché but it isn't. The powerful silhouette of Gustave Eiffel's marvel of engineering still makes a stirring sight, especially at night when its delicate, lace-like iron structure comes to the fore.

Glittering feat Built in a record two years for the 1889 Exposition Universelle, the controversial Eiffel Tower was never intended to be a permanent feature of the city. However, in 1910 it was finally saved for posterity, so preparing the way for today's 6 million annual visitors. Avoid a long wait for the lift by visiting the tower at night, when it fully lives up to its romantic image and provides a glittering spectacle—whether the 352,000-watt illumination of the tower known as the staircase to infinity, or the carpet of nocturnal Paris unfolding at its feet.

Violent reactions Gustave Eiffel was a master of cast-iron structures, his prolific output including hundreds of factories, churches, viaducts and bridges on four continents. His 320-m (1,050-ft) tower attracted great opposition, but his genius was vindicated by the fact that it sways no more

than 6–7cm (2.5in) in high winds and remained the world's highest structure for 40 years. Eiffel kept an office here until his death in 1923; he may have seen Comte de Lambert circle above in a flying-machine in 1909, or a modern-day Icarus plummet to his death from the parapet in 1912.

Champs Élysées & Arc de Triomphe

You may not be enamoured of fast-food outlets and airline offices, both of which are major features of this once-glamorous avenue. But a facelift has upgraded it, enhancing the magnificent east–west perspective.

Slow start It was Marie de Médicis, wife of Henri IV, who first made this a fashionable boulevard in 1616, but it was the celebrated landscape designer André Le Nôtre who contributed to its name—Elysian Fields—by planting alleys of trees and gardens. The heyday came in 1824 when new walkways and fountains made it the most fashionable promenading spot in Paris, with cafés and restaurants catering to a well-heeled clientele. The crowning glory was the Arc de Triomphe (▶ 59), commissioned by Napoleon, while the 1900 Exposition Universelle added The Grand Palais (which includes the Palais de la Découverte) and the Petit Palais at the lower end. The Grand Palais now hosts high profile temporary art exhibitions, while the Palais de la Découverte has a science museum and planetarium.

Parades Despite being dominated by commercial and tourist facilities, the Champs Élysées remains the focal point for national ceremonies, whether the 14 July military parade, Armistice Day's wreath-laying at the Arc de Triomphe or the fast-pedalling *grande finale* of the Tour de France. When France won the World Cup in 1998, the Champs Élysées was packed with fans.

Luxury These days the Champs Élysées may be dominated by car showrooms, but plush cinemas, classy shops and one or two fashionable watering holes still remain to tempt those who want to see and be seen.

HIGHLIGHTS

- Arc de Triomphe
- Rude's *La Marseillaise* sculpture on Arc de Triomphe
- L'Étoile
- Bluebell Girls at Lido
- Le Fouquet's restaurant
- Palais de l'Élysée
- Grand Palais
- Philatelists' market

INFORMATION

- C3–F4; B2; Locator map A2–B2
- Champs Élysées 75008
- Grand Palais 01 44 13 17 17; Petit Palais (closed for renovation until late 2005) 01 44 51 19 31; Palais de la Découverte 01 56 43 20 21; www.paris.fr/musees and www.palais-decouverte.fr
- Grand Palais Wed–Mon 10–8, (10 on Wed); Palais de la Découverte Tue–Sat 9.30–6, Sun 10–7
- Grand Palais cafeteria; restaurants on Champs Élysées (mainly at the Arc de Triomphe end)
- Charles de Gaulle-Étoile, Georges V, Franklin D. Roosevelt, Champs-Élysées-Clémenceau
- 28, 72, 83, 93
- Good
- Grand Palais expensive; Palais de la Découverte moderate

Les Invalides

HIGHLIGHTS

- 196-m (643-ft) façade
- Sword and armour of François I
- Napoleon's stuffed horse
- *Emperor Napoleon*, Ingres
- Napoleon's tomb
- Église du Dôme
- A Renault light tank
- Dragon mask in oriental collection
- World War II exhibition

INFORMATION

www.invalides.org

- E7–F7; Locator map B3
- ✉ 129 rue de Grenelle 75007
- ☎ Musée de l'Armée 01 44 42 38 77
- 🕐 Apr–end Sep daily 10–6; Oct–end Mar 10–5
  Église du Dôme mid-Jun to mid-Sep daily 10–6.45
- 🚇 La Tour Maubourg, Invalides, Varenne
- 🚌 28, 63, 83, 93
- 🚆 RER Line C Invalides
- ♿ Partial access
- 💵 Moderate
- ↔ Musée Rodin (► 31)
- ❓ Guided tours on request (01 44 42 37 72).
  Renovation work means some rooms are temporarily closed

The gilded dome rising above the Hôtel des Invalides recalls the pomp and glory of France's two greatest promoters—the Sun King, who built it, and the power-hungry Napoleon Bonaparte, who is entombed there.

Glory The vast, imposing edifice of Les Invalides was built to house invalid soldiers, and it continues to accommodate a few today. Its classical façade and majestic Cour d'Honneur date from the 1670s, with the ornate Église du Dôme completed in 1706 and the long grassy esplanade established soon after. The home of military institutions, Les Invalides is also a memorial to the succession of battles and campaigns that have marked French history and which are illustrated in the Musée de l'Armée. Here is Napoleon's frock coat and his actual horse, Vizir, (not for the squeamish). You can also see the armour of François I and the intriguing oriental collection complete with a dragon mask for horses. The

The Cour d'Honneur

World War II exhibition is particularly poignant.

Tombs The baroque cupolas, arches, columns and sculptures of the Église du Dôme highlight France's military achievements and heroes. Tombs of generals fill the chapels while the crypt contains Napoleon's grandiose sarcophagus guarded by 12 statues, symbols of his military campaigns.

Musée Rodin

As a complete antidote to the military might of Les Invalides, wander into the enchanting Musée Rodin, often forgotten by Parisians. This peaceful enclave is a good escape from the hurly-burly of the boulevards.

Hard times This rococo mansion, built for a prosperous wig-maker in 1730, has a checkered history. One owner (the Duc de Lauzun) was sent to the guillotine, and the house has been used successively as a dance hall, convent, school and as artists' studios. Rodin lived here from 1908 until his death in 1917, with such neighbours as the poet Rainer Maria Rilke and dancer Isadora Duncan. In 1919 the house was turned into a museum.

Sculpture The elegant, luminous interior houses the collection of works that Rodin left to the nation. It ranges from his early academic sketches to the later watercolours, and displays many of his most celebrated white marble and bronze sculptures, including *The Kiss* (Le Baiser). There are busts of the composer Mahler, the suffragette Eva Fairfax and Victor Hugo to name but a few, as well as a series of studies of Balzac in paunchy splendour. Alongside the Rodins are works by his contemporaries, in particular his tragic mistress and model, Camille Claudel, as well as Eugène Carrière, Edvard Munch, Renoir, Monet and van Gogh. Rodin's furniture and antiques complete this exceptional collection.

Retreat The museum's private gardens are Paris's third largest and contain several major sculptures, a pond, flowering shrubs and benches for a quiet read. It's worth buying the garden-only ticket just for a respite from city life.

HIGHLIGHTS

- *Les Bourgeois de Calais*
- *Le Penseur*
- *La Porte de l'Enfer*
- *Le Baiser*
- *La Main de Dieu*
- *Saint Jean Baptiste*
- *Adam et Eve*
- *Ugolin*
- *Le Père Tanguy*, van Gogh
- Original staircase

INFORMATION

www.musee-rodin.fr
- F7; Locator map C3
- 77 rue de Varenne 75007
- 01 44 18 61 10
- Apr–end Sep Tue–Sun 9.30–5.45; Oct–end Mar 9.30–4.45 (gardens stay open until 6.45 in summer; last entry at 5.15)
- Peaceful garden café
- Varenne
- 69, 82, 87, 92
- Wheelchair access at ground level and garden
- Inexpensive
- Les Invalides (➤ 30)

Place de la Concorde

DID YOU KNOW?

- The Egyptian obelisk weighs 254 tonnes
- 133 people were trampled to death here in 1770
- 1,300 heads were guillotined here in 1793–95

INFORMATION

- G5; Locator map C2
- place de la Concorde 75008
- Jeu de Paume 01 47 03 12 50
- Jeu de Paume Wed–Fri noon–7, Tue noon–9.30, Sat–Sun 10–7
- Small café in Jeu de Paume
- Concorde
- 24, 42, 52, 72, 73, 84, 94
- Jeu de Paume excellent
- Jeu de Paume moderate
- Champs Élysées & Arc de Triomphe (➤ 29), Jardin des Tuileries (➤ 58)
- Jeu de Paume annexe in Hôtel de Sully, 62 rue Saint-Antoine
  - St-Paul

As you stand in this noisy traffic-choked square it is hard to imagine the crowds baying for the deaths of Marie-Antoinette and Louis XVI, who were both guillotined here at the height of the French Revolution.

Chop-chop This pulsating square was initially laid out in the mid-18th century to accommodate a statue of King Louis XV. Under the new name of place de la Révolution it then witnessed the mass executions of the French Revolution, and was finally renamed the place de la Concorde in 1795 as revolutionary zeal abated. In the 19th century, Guillaume Coustou's *Chevaux de Marly* were erected at the base of the Champs Élysées (today reproductions; the originals now housed in the Louvre). Crowning the middle of the Concorde is a 3,000-year-old Egyptian obelisk overlooking eight symbolic statues of French cities. Use the pedestrian crossing to reach the central island and get a closer look at the obelisk framed by two romantic fountains.

Grandeur To the north, bordering the rue Royale, stand the colonnaded Hôtel Crillon (on the left) and the matching Hôtel de la Marine (right), both relics from pre-Revolution days. The rue Royale itself, with its luxury establishments, leads to the Madeleine. The eastern side of the Concorde is dominated by two public art galleries. The Jeu de Paume (by rue de Rivoli), restructured in 2004, is now exclusively focused on the art of photography. The Orangerie (nearer the river) is famous for its impressive basement panels of Monet's *Water Lilies* (closed for refurbishing until mid-2006). Visible across the bridge to the south is the Palais Bourbon, home to the Assemblée Nationale (French parliament).

Musée d'Orsay

You'll either love or hate the conversion of this 1900 train station, but whatever your view its art collections, covering the years from 1848 to 1914, are a must for anyone interested in this crucial art period.

Monolithic When this museum finally opened in 1986 controversy ran high: Gae Aulenti's heavy stone structures lay unhappily under Laloux's delicate iron and glass shell, built as a train terminus in 1900. But the collections redeem this *faux pas*, offering a solid overview of the momentous period from Romanticism to Fauvism. After exploring the 19th-century paintings, sculptures and decorative arts at

The Church at Auvers, *van Gogh*

ground level, take the escalator to the upper floor. Here the Pont-Aven and the Impressionist schools are displayed along with the giants of French art—Degas, Monet, Cézanne, van Gogh, Renoir, Sisley and Pissaro. This level is the biggest crowd puller. And don't miss the views from the outside terrace and café behind the station clock at the top.

And finally The middle level is devoted to painting (Symbolism, Naturalism and the Nabis) and sculpture from 1870 to 1914, and includes works by Rodin, Émile-Antoine Bourdelle and Astride Maillol. Art-nouveau furniture is also displayed.

HIGHLIGHTS

- *Olympia,* Manet
- *Déjeuner sur l'Herbe,* Manet
- *Orphée,* Gustave Moreau
- *La Mère,* Whistler
- *L'Angélus du Soir,* Millet
- *La Cathédrale de Rouen,* Monet
- *L'Absinthe,* Degas
- *La Chambre à Arles,* van Gogh
- *Femmes de Tahiti,* Gauguin
- Chair by Charles Rennie Mackintosh

INFORMATION

www.musee-orsay.fr

⊞ H6; Locator map C3

✉ 1 rue de la Légion d'honneur

☎ 01 40 49 48 00 or 01 40 49 49 78

🕓 Tue–Sat 10–6, Sun 9–6, Thu 10–9.45 (opens at 9, late Jun–late Sep)

🍴 Café des Hauteurs on upper level; snack bar above plush restaurant/ tea room on middle level

Ⓜ Solférino

🚌 24, 63, 68, 69, 73, 83, 84, 94

🚆 RER Line C Musée d'Orsay

♿ Excellent

💷 Moderate; free first Sun of each month

❓ Self-guided audio and guided tours, concerts and lectures

Opéra de Paris Garnier

This is an ornate wedding cake of a building, but the sumptuous and riotous details that decorate its every surface are in fact the perfect epitaph to the frenetic architectural activities of the Second Empire.

HIGHLIGHTS

- Grand Staircase
- Grand Foyer
- Auditorium
- Façade
- Lamp-bearers

DID YOU KNOW?

- Garnier's design was selected from 171 others
- The total surface area of the building is 11,000sq m (118,400sq ft)
- The auditorium holds 2,200 spectators
- The stage accommodates over 450 performers

INFORMATION

www.opera-de-paris.fr
- J3; Locator map D2
- place de l'Opéra 75009
- Information, reservations and tours 0892 89 90 90
- Daily 10–4.30
- Bar open during shows
- Opéra
- 20, 21, 22, 27, 29, 42, 52, 53, 66, 68, 81, 95
- RER Auber
- Few, call for appointment
- Moderate
- Place de la Concorde (► 32)
- Guided tours in English on Sat–Sun at 12.30
  01 41 10 08 10

Past glory When Charles Garnier's opera house was inaugurated in 1875 it marked the end of Haussmann's ambitious urban facelift and announced the sociocultural movement to the belle-époque, with Nijinksy and Diaghilev's Ballets Russes as later highlights. Today the Salle Garnier mostly stages dance with only some opera, many prestigious operatic performances having been switched to the Opéra Bastille when the latter opened in 1989. Rudolf Nureyev was director of the Paris Ballet here between 1983 and 1989, and this was where he first danced in the West. Nureyev was succeeded by Patrick Dupond whose brilliant career prompted him to leave the Opéra in 1998. He was followed by Brigitte Lefèvre.

Dazzle Competing with a series of provocative lamp-bearing statues, the Palais Garnier's extravagant, regilded façade of arches, winged horses, friezes and columns is topped by a verdigris dome and leads into a majestic foyer. This is dominated by the Grand Staircase, dripping with balconies and chandeliers, in turn sweeping upwards to the Grand Foyer and its gilded mirrors, marble, murals and Murano glass. Do not miss the equally ornate auditorium, with its dazzling gold-leaf decorations and red-velvet seats, and Marc Chagall's incongruous false ceiling, painted in 1964. The Opéra is open outside rehearsals; enter through Riccardo Pedruzzi's 1990s library and the museum of operatic memorabilia.

Sacré Cœur

Few people would admit it, but the high point of a trip up here is not the basilica itself but the stunning views. You can't forget, however, that Sacré Cœur was built in honour of the 58,000 dead of the Franco-Prussian War.

Weighty Although construction started in 1875, it was not until 1914 that this white neo-Romanesque-Byzantine edifice was completed, partly due to the problems of laying foundations in the quarry-riddled hill of Montmartre. Priests still work in relays to maintain the tradition of perpetual prayer for forgiveness of the horrors of war and for the massacre of some 20,000 Communards by government troops. The

square bell tower was an afterthought and houses one of the world's heaviest bells, La Savoyarde, which weighs in at 21 tonnes. The stained-glass windows are replacements of those that were shattered by enemy bombs in 1944.

Byzantine mosaic of Christ, chancel vault

Panoramas This unmistakable feature of the Paris skyline magnetises the crowds arriving either by funicular or via the steep steps of the terraced garden. Dawn and dusk offer sparkling panoramas over the city, especially from the exterior terrace of the dome, the second-highest point in Paris after the Eiffel Tower (access is from the left-hand side of the basilica). Just to the west of Sacré Cœur is the diminutive Saint-Pierre, a much reworked though charming church that is all that remains of the Benedictine abbey of Montmartre founded in 1133.

HIGHLIGHTS

- La Savoyarde bell
- View from the dome
- Mosaic of Christ
- Treasure of Sacré Cœur
- Bronze doors at Saint-Pierre
- Stained-glass gallery
- Statue of Christ
- Statue of Virgin Mary and Child
- The funicular ride from place Saint-Pierre
- Hearing the choir sing during a service

INFORMATION

www.sacre-coeur-montmartre.com

➕ Montmartre map; Locator map E1

✉ place du Parvis du Sacré Coeur, 75018

☎ 01 53 41 89 00;

🕐 Basilica daily 6.45am–11pm; dome and crypt 9–6 (also until 7 in summer)

🚇 Abbesses (from here, walk along rue Yvonne Le Tac and rue Tardieu, then take funicular or walk up steps)

🚌 Montmartrobus

♿ Wheelchair access from the back of the basilica

🎟 Basilica free; dome and crypt inexpensive

Musée des Arts Décoratifs

INFORMATION

www.ucad.fr

- J5; Locator map D2
- 107 rue de Rivoli 75001
- 01 44 55 57 50
- Tue–Fri 11–6, Sat–Sun 10–6
- Palais-Royal, Musée du Louvre
- 21, 27, 39, 48, 69, 72, 81, 95
- Excellent
- Inexpensive
- Musée du Louvre (► 37)

The discreet old-fashioned atmosphere of this fascinating museum devoted to interior design and decoration was blown away by President Mitterrand's *grand projet* that swept right through the Louvre palace.

Looking back The Musée des Arts Décoratifs is one of four museums forming the Union Centrale des Arts Décoratifs founded at the end of the 19th century by a group of industrialists and collectors wishing to exhibit 'Beauty in function'. Throughout the 20th century contributions by designers such as Le Corbusier, Mallet-Stevens, Nikki de Saint Phalle and Philippe Starck greatly enriched the collections. Extensive renovation of the museum, housed since 1905 in the Marsan wing of the Louvre, is due to complete in 2005; only the medieval and Renaissance department are currently open.

Medieval and Renaissance Department The exotic collections, spanning the 13th to the 16th century, are displayed with stunning effect in nine rooms where religious paintings, sculptures and furniture contrast with exquisite objects of daily life. The Galerie des Retables contains remarkable examples of altarpieces in carved wood or stone from all over Europe. One room is named after the Maître de la Madeleine, a 13th-century Italian painter, whose *Virgin and Child between St. Andrew and St. James* is proudly displayed among other works ranging from the primitive to the late Gothic style. The Salle des Vitraux has beautiful 16th-century stained glass, while a selection of tapestries is exhibited in rotation in the Salle des Tapisseries. The Galerie des Bijoux, opened in June 2004, presents a fascinating display of jewellery from the Middle Ages until the present day.

Top: A richly decorated 16th-century carpet from India

Musée du Louvre

Nocturnal lighting transforms the Louvre's glass pyramid entrance into a gigantic cut diamond—just a foretaste of the treasures contained within. The state-of-the-art renovation is just the icing on the cake.

The world's largest museum Since 1981 the Louvre has been undergoing a radical transformation (due for completion in 2005) that crowns six centuries of eventful existence. As a fitting culmination of the project, the museum's star attraction, the Mona Lisa, will move to a room that has been specially refurbished to make viewing the painting easier. Originally a medieval castle, the Louvre first took shape as an art gallery under François I, eager to display his Italian loot. Catherine de Médicis transformed it into a palace in 1578. After escaping the excesses of the revolutionary mob, in 1793 it became a people's museum and was later further enlarged by Napoleon I, who also greatly enriched its collection.

Mona Lisa, *Leonardo da Vinci*

Art fortress The vast collection of some 30,000 exhibits is arranged on four floors of three wings: Sully (east), Richelieu (north) and Denon (south), while beneath the elegant Cour Carrée lie the keep and dungeons of the original medieval fortress. Almost 5,000 years of art are covered, starting with Egyptian antiquities and culminating with European painting up to 1848.

HIGHLIGHTS

- Palace of Khorsabad
- Glass pyramid entrance, designed by I. M. Pei
- *Bataille de San Romano,* Uccello
- *Mona Lisa,* da Vinci
- *La Dentellière,* Vermeer
- *Vénus de Milo*
- Cour Carrée at night

INFORMATION

- 🗺 K6; Locator map D2
- ✉ 99 rue de Rivoli 75001
- ☎ 01 40 20 53 17; Auditorium 01 40 20 55 55
- 🕐 Wed–Mon 9–6 (until 9.45pm Wed, Fri)
- 🍴 Wide selection of restaurants and cafés
- Ⓜ Palais-Royal, Musée du Louvre
- 🚌 21, 27, 39, 48,67, 68, 69, 72, 74, 75, 76, 81, 85, 95
- ♿ Excellent
- 💰 Moderate until 6pm; inexpensive after 6pm on late nights and Sun; free first Sun of every month
- 🔁 Musée des Arts Décoratifs (► 36),
- ❓ Guided tours and audio-guides, regular lectures, films, workshops, concerts in auditorium. To avoid a long wait, buy your ticket via the Internet: www.louvre.fr or at Virgin megastore in the Carrousel du Louvre precinct

Galeries Vivienne & Colbert

DID YOU KNOW?

- Explorer Bougainville lived here
- Revolutionary Simón Bolívar lived here
- Crook-turned-cop Vidocq lived here in the 1840s

INFORMATION

- L4; Locator map D2
- Galerie Vivienne & Galerie Colbert 75002
- Gate at 5 rue de la Banque is open from 8am–9pm
- Bourse, Palais-Royal, Musée du Louvre
- 29
- Good
- Free
- Jardin du Palais-Royal (➤ 61)

These connecting 19th-century passages, with their original mosaic floors and neoclassical decoration, are a perfect place for people-watching, offering a complete contrast to the trendy buzz of neighbouring streets.

Shopping arcades Between the late 18th and early 19th centuries the Right Bank included a network of 140 covered passageways—the fashionable shopping malls of the time. Today there are fewer than 30, of which the Galeries Vivienne and Colbert are perhaps the best known, squeezed in between the Bibliothèque Nationale and the place des Victoires. Bookworms and fashion-victims cross paths in this elegant, skylit setting lined with potted palms, where there is also the occasional fashion show. It is perfect for a rainy day browse.

Hive of interest The Galerie Vivienne (1823) opens onto three different streets, while the parallel Galerie Colbert (1826) has its own entrances. Colbert is now an annexe of the Bibliothèque Nationale, and regular exhibitions (prints, photos, theatre accessories) and concerts are held in its galleries and auditorium. Galerie Vivienne is commercial in spirit: This is where you can track down designer watches, antiquarian or rare artists' books (bookshop established in 1826 at Nos. 45 and 46), contemporary design, fine wines, intriguing toys, or just sit sipping tea beneath the skylight, watching the world go by.

The mosaic floor (top) and the bronze statue (right) in the Galerie Vivienne

Jardin du Luxembourg

Despite the crowds, these gardens are serene in all weather and are the epitome of French landscaping. The occupants present an idealized image of an unhurried Parisian existence far from the daily truth of noise and traffic.

Layout Radiating from the large octagonal pond in front of the Palais du Luxembourg (now the Senate) are terraces, paths and a wide tree-lined alley that leads down to the Observatory crossroads. Natural attractions include shady chestnuts, potted orange and palm trees, lawns and even an experimental fruit garden and orchard, while fountains, tennis courts, bee-hives, a puppet theatre and children's playgrounds offer other distractions. Statues of the queens of France, artists and writers are dotted about the terraces and avenues. A plaque marks the tree planted in memory of the victims of 11 September 2001.

Park activities All year round joggers work off their *foie gras* on the circumference, and in summer sunbathers and bookworms settle into park chairs, card- and chess-playing retirees claim the shade in front of the palace, bands tune up at the bandstand near the boulevard Saint-Michel entrance and children burn off energy on swings and donkey rides.

Inspiration The Palais du Luxembourg and surrounding garden were originally commissioned by Marie de Médicis, wife of Henri IV, in 1615, and designed to resemble her childhood Florentine home. The Allée de l'Observatoire and the English-style garden were added in the early 19th century. A petition signed by 12,000 Parisians luckily saved the garden from Haussmann's urban ambitions.

HIGHLIGHTS

- Médicis fountain
- Cyclops, Acis and Galateus sculptures
- Bandstand
- Statue of Delacroix
- Orange-tree conservatory
- Experimental fruit garden
- Beekeeping school
- Statues of queens of France

DID YOU KNOW?

- Isadora Duncan danced here
- Ernest Hemingway claimed to capture pigeons here for his supper

INFORMATION

- K10; Locator map D4
- Main entrance at boulevard Saint-Michel, 75006 (various entries around the park)
- Senate 01 42 34 20 00; www.senat.fr
- Apr–end Oct daily 7.30am–9.30pm; Nov–end Mar 8.15–5 (times may vary)
- Open-air cafés, kiosk restaurant
- Odéon
- RER Luxembourg
- 21, 27, 38, 58, 82, 84, 85, 89
- Very good Free
- Église Saint-Sulpice (► 54)

39

Musée de Cluny

INFORMATION

www.musee-moyenage.fr

L9; Locator map E3

6 place Paul-Painlevé 75005

01 53 73 78 00

Wed–Mon 9.15–5.45

Cluny-La Sorbonne

21, 27, 38, 63, 85, 86, 87, 96

Inexpensive

Sainte Chapelle (➤ 41)

Guided tours of vaults, baths and collections: information and reservation

01 53 73 78 16

Take a deep breath outside the Musée de Cluny, surrounded by newly-created medieval gardens, and prepare to enter a time warp in which the days of the troubadours and courtly love are re-created in its panelled rooms.

Baths The late 2nd-century Roman baths adjoining the Hôtel de Cluny are composed of three stone chambers: the Caldarium (steam bath), the Tepidarium (tepid bath) and the Frigidarium (cold bath), with ruins of the former gymnasium visible on the boulevard Saint-Germain side. Important Roman stonework is exhibited in the niches, while Room VIII houses 21 mutilated heads from Notre Dame. Recent excavations have also opened up a labyrinth of Roman vaults that can be toured with a guide.

Treasures The Gothic turreted mansion was built in 1500 by the abbot Jacques d'Amboise and is one of France's finest examples of domestic architecture of this period. Some 23,000 objects compose the collection, much of which was gathered by the 19th-century medievalist and collector, Alexandre du Sommerard. Perhaps the most famous piece is the beautiful *La Dame à la Licorne* tapestry, woven in the late 15th century. Six enigmatic panels depict a woman, a lion and a unicorn, animals, flowers and birds, all exquisitely worked. Costumes, accessories, textiles and tapestries are of Byzantine, Coptic or European origin, while the gold and metalwork room houses some outstanding pieces of Gallic, Barbarian, Merovingian and Visigothic artistry. Stained glass, table games, ceramics, wood carvings, illuminated manuscripts and Books of Hours, altarpieces and religious statuary complete this exceptional and very manageable display.

Top: À mon Seul Désir, *one of the* La Dame à la Licorne *tapestries*

Sainte Chapelle

Sainte Chapelle's spire, soaring 75m (246ft) above the ground, is in itself a great expression of faith, but inside this is surpassed by the glowing intensity of the stained-glass windows reaching up to a star-studded roof.

Masterpiece One of Paris's oldest and most significant monuments stands within the precincts of the Palais de Justice. The chapel was built by Louis IX (later canonized) to house relics he had acquired at exorbitant cost during the crusades, and which included what was reputed to be the Crown of Thorns, as well as fragments of the

Cross and drops of Christ's blood (now kept in Notre Dame). Pierre de Montreuil masterminded this delicate Gothic construction, bypassing the use of flying buttresses, incorporating a lower chapel for palace servants to worship and installing 670sq m (7, 209sq ft) of striking

stained glass above. Completed in 1248 in record time, it served as Louis IX's private chapel with discreet access from what was then the royal palace.

Apocalypse More than 1,000 biblical scenes are illustrated in the 16 windows, starting with Genesis in the window to the left of the entrance, and working round the chapel to finish with the Apocalypse, in the rose window. The statues of the Apostles are mostly copies—the damaged originals are at the Musée de Cluny.

HIGHLIGHTS

- Rose window
- Oratory
- 19th-century restoration
- Tombs of canons
- Stained-glass depiction of Christ's Passion
- Saint Louis himself in the 'Story of the Relics' window

INFORMATION

www.monum.fr
- M8; Locator map E3
- 4 boulevard du Palais 75001
- 01 53 40 60 80
- Daily 9.30–6
- Cité, St-Michel
- 21, 24, 38, 85, 96
- RER Line B, St-Michel
- Moderate (joint ticket with the Conciergerie moderate)
- Musée de Cluny (➤ 40)
- To help make sense of the windows, pick up an information card from the stand near the exit. Guided tours daily at 11 and 3

Top: The stained-glass windows of the upper chapel

41

Conciergerie

DID YOU KNOW?

- 288 prisoners were massacred here in 1792
- 4,164 citizens were held here during the Terror
- Comte d'Armagnac was assassinated here
- 22 left-wing Girondins were held in one room
- Robespierre spent his last night
- Charles V commissioned Paris' first public clock to sit on the Tour de l'Horloge in 1370

INFORMATION

www.monum.fr

- M7; Locator map E3
- 2 boulevard du Palais 75001
- 01 53 73 78 50 or 01 53 40 60 93
- Daily 9.30–6; closed public holidays
- Cité, Châtelet
- 21, 24, 38, 85, 96
- Moderate (joint ticket with Sainte Chapelle moderate)
- Sainte Chapelle (▶ 41)
- Guided tours daily

Top: Salle des Gens d'Armes

The ghosts of the victims of the guillotine must surely haunt this stark and gloomy place that served as a prison and torture chamber for over five centuries, and remains full of macabre mementos of its grisly past.

From Palace to Prison Rising over the Seine in menacing splendour, the turreted Conciergerie was built from 1299 to 1313 as part of a royal complex that also included Sainte Chapelle. From 1391 until 1914 the building functioned as a prison and torture chamber, its reputation striking fear into the hearts of the population. During the Revolution more than 4,000 prisoners were held here. Many never tasted freedom again, including Marie-Antoinette, wife of Louis XVI.

Re-live History The boulevard du Palais entrance takes you into the hauntingly lit Salle des Gens d'Armes. This is thought to be one of Europe's oldest surviving medieval halls, and is where members of the royal household once ate their meals. From here a curious spiral staircase leads to the original kitchens. Off the Salle des Gens d'Armes is the gloomy Salle des Gardes. This sat underneath the Grand' Chambre, where the Revolutionary court dealt out countless death sentences. Across the corridor known as the rue de Paris is the Galerie des Prisonniers, where lawyers, prisoners and visitors mingled. Here you can see a re-creation of the Concierge's and clerk's offices, as well as the Salle de Toilette, where prisoners were prepared for execution. At the far end is a poignant re-creation of Marie-Antoinette's cell. The eerie upstairs corridor has examples of the three types of cell available to prisoners, depending on their wealth. Another room lists the guillotine's 2,278 victims.

Centre Georges Pompidou

Late opening hours make an exhibition visit possible between an aperitif and dinner in this still-controversial cultural centre. You can take your pick between the genesis of modernism, an art film or a drama performance.

High-tech culture More than a mere landmark in the extensive facelift that Paris has undergone since the 1970s, the high-tech Centre Pompidou (known to Parisians as Beaubourg) is a hive of changing cultural activity. Contemporary art, architecture, design, photography, theatre, cinema and dance are all represented, while the lofty structure itself offers exceptional views over

central Paris. Take the transparent escalator tubes for a bird's-eye view of the piazza where jugglers, artists, musicians and portrait artists ply their trades to the teeming crowds.

The fountain in nearby place Igor Stravinsky

Facelift The Centre Pompidou has been completely renovated for the new millenium. The permanent collections of the Musée National d'Art Moderne are on levels 4 and 5. Levels 1, 4 and 6 are for temporary exhibitions, while a public information library is located on levels 1, 2 and 3. The ground level includes a bookshop (other boutiques on levels, 1, 4 and 6), a post office and a children's workshop. There are cinemas on the first and lower floors and the restaurant Georges (► 64), with its wonderful views over the city, is on the top floor.

HIGHLIGHTS

- Design by Richard Rogers, Renzo Piano and Jean-François Bodin
- View from the escalator
- Stravinsky fountain
- *The Deep,* Jackson Pollock
- *Phoque,* Brancusi
- *Bleu II,* Miró
- *Infiltration homogène,* Joseph Beuys
- Gouache cut-outs, Matisse
- *Improvisations,* Kandinsky

INFORMATION

www.centrepompidou.fr

- N6; Locator map E2
- place Georges-Pompidou
- 01 44 78 12 33
- Wed–Mon 11–10. Museum and exhibits 11–9; Brancusi Workshop Wed–Mon 2–6; Library Mon, Wed–Fri noon–10, Sat, Sun 11–10
- Georges restaurant on 6th floor; café on 1st floor
- Rambuteau, Hôtel de Ville
- 38, 47, 67, 75, 76
- RER Line A, B, Châtelet-Les Halles
- Excellent
- Permanent collections moderate; full ticket expensive
- Frequent lectures, concerts, parallel activities, Atelier des Enfants

43

Marché aux Puces de Saint-Ouen

INFORMATION

www.antikita.com
- Off map at J1; Locator map off C1
- Porte de Clignancourt
- Sat–Mon 9–6
- Cafés and restaurants on rue des Rosiers. A. Picolo ☎ 01 40 11 11 19
- Porte de Clignancourt
- 56, 85
- Good
- Free
- Sacré Cœur (► 35)
- Beware of pickpockets

A Sunday pastime favoured by many locals is to look for bargains at the city's flea markets, of which the crème de la crème is still this one. Nowhere else will you find such a fascinating cross-section of Parisian society.

Duck and banter The approach from the Métro to this sprawling 7-ha (17-acre) market is uninspiring as it entails bypassing household goods, jeans and shoe stalls before ducking under the *Périphérique* overpass and finally entering the fray. Persevere and you may discover an antique gem, a fake or a second-hand pilot's jacket. If your budget won't stretch to that you can choose an old postcard of Paris from the thousands on show. Everything and anything is displayed here but all commerce is carried on in the true bantering style of the *faubourgs*, a habit that dates from the late 19th century when the first junkmen moved in to offer their wares for sale.

Bargain Registered dealers are divided into over a dozen official markets that interconnect through passageways bustling with crowds. Along the fringes are countless hopefuls who set up temporary stands to sell a mind-boggling range of goods from obsolete kitchenware to old jukeboxes and cheap junk. Although unashamedly a tourist trap, there is something for everyone here, but do go early. Bargaining is obligatory and prices are directly related to the weather: high on sunny, crowded days and low under cold, wet skies. Stop for lunch in one of the animated bistros along the rue des Rosiers or try the terrace of A. Picolo at 58 rue Jules-Vallès. On weekends as many as 150,000 bargain-hunters, tourists and dealers can cram the passageways—avoid Sunday afternoons in particular, when crowds and pickpockets abound.

Notre Dame

Spectacular is the word to describe Paris's most extraordinary monument, with its 90-m (295-ft) spire and world-renowned flying buttresses. One of the finest views of the cathedral is from the *quais* to the east.

Evolution Construction started on this labour of faith in 1163 but it was not finished until 1345, making it range in style between Romanesque and Gothic. Since then the cathedral has suffered from pollution, politics, aesthetic trends and religious change. Louis XV declared stained glass outmoded and replaced most of the rose windows with clear glass (the stained glass was later restored), Revolutionary anticlericalism toppled countless statues and the spire was amputated in 1787. Not least, Viollet-le-Duc, the fervent 19th-century medievalist architect, was let loose on its restoration and initiated radical alterations.

Interior grandeur The hushed, softly lit stone interior contains numerous chapels, tombs and statues, as well as the sacristy (south side of choir) where the treasure of Notre Dame is kept. Climb the towers—386 steps—for fantastic views and a close-up of the gargoyles. Look closely at the three asymmetrical sculpted portals on the façade: These once served as a Bible for illiterate worshippers. Finally, walk round the cathedral for a view of its extravagant flying buttresses.

HIGHLIGHTS

- Views from the towers
- South rose window
- Porte Rouge
- Portail du Cloître
- The gargoyles
- Emmanuel bell
- 1730 organ
- *Pietà*, Coustou
- Statue of Notre Dame de Paris
- 14th-century Virgin and Child

INFORMATION

- M8; Locator map E3
- place du Parvis Notre Dame 75004
- 01 42 34 56 10; crypt 01 55 42 50 10
- Cathedral Mon–Fri 8–6.45, Sat–Sun 8–7.45; closed on some feast days. Tower Apr–end Sep daily 9.30–7.30 (also until 11pm, Sat–Sun, Jul–end Aug); Oct–end Mar 10–5.30. Treasure Mon–Sat 9.30–11.30, 1–5.30
- Cité, St-Michel
- 24, 47
- RER Lines B and C, St-Michel
- Good (but not in towers)
- Cathedral free; tower moderate; treasure inexpensive

The southern aspect of Notre Dame, showing the south rose window (detail above)

Île Saint-Louis

HIGHLIGHTS

- Église Saint-Louis-en-l'Île
- Doorway of Hôtel de Chenizot and Hôtel Lambert, rue Saint-Louis-en-l'Île
- Hôtel Lambert
- Camille Claudel's home and studio, 19 quai de Bourbon
- Square Barye
- Brasserie de l'Île Saint-Louis
- Pont Marie
- High-water mark, 1 quai d'Anjou
- Berthillon, 31 rue Saint-Louis-en-l'Île

INFORMATION

- N8–P9; Locator map F3
- Sunny terrace of La Brasserie de l'Île
- Pont Marie, Sully Morland
- 67, 86, 87
- Good
- Notre Dame (➤ 45)

Floating mid-Seine is this fascinating residential island, a living museum of 17th-century architecture and also a popular tourist haunt. You may spot an illustrious resident, but above all indulge in the island's own ice cream.

History Once a marshy swamp, the Île Saint-Louis was transformed into an elegant residential area in the 17th century, when it was joined to the

Courtyard, quai de Bourbon

Île de la Cité. Today, bridges link it to the Right Bank and the Left Bank, but nevertheless it still maintains a spirit of its own, and residents openly boast that its food shops are unsurpassable. Cutting across it lengthwise is rue Saint-Louis-en-l'Île lined with upmarket groceries, arts and craft shops and restaurants. It is also home to the Église Saint-Louis-en-l'Île, begun by Le Vau in 1664. The side streets here are mainly residential.

Hashish The Quai d'Anjou, on the northeast side, has a rich past. Former residents include the architect himself, Le Vau, at No. 3, Honoré Daumier (No. 9), Baudelaire and Théophile Gautier who, at No. 17, animated his Club des Haschichins. Commemorative plaques to the famous pepper the façades of the island's harmonious townhouses, and the riverside paths offer quintessential Parisian views, romantic trysts and summer sunbathing. Before leaving, make sure you try a Berthillon ice cream, reputedly the best in the world.

Institut du Monde Arabe

It is difficult to miss this gleaming, ultracontemporary building as you cross the Seine. Although some may find it limited, the museum's collection does offer a sleekly presented introduction to Islamic culture.

Arab inspiration Clean lines, aluminum walls and glass are the hallmarks of the design for the Arab Institute, which was inaugurated in 1987 to foster cultural exchange between Islamic countries and the West. Innovative features include high-speed transparent elevators, a system of high-tech metal screens on the south elevation that filter light entering the institute and which were inspired by the *moucharabiehs* (carved wooden screens) on traditional Arab buildings and an enclosed courtyard achieved by splitting the building in two. The institute's facilities comprise a museum, library, exhibition halls, audiovisual facilities and an elegant rooftop restaurant boasting spectacular panoramas across the Seine.

Museum First take the lift to the 9th floor for sweeping views across the Île Saint-Louis and northeastern Paris, then head down to the museum on the 7th floor. Here, finely crafted metalwork, ceramics, textiles, carpets and calligraphy reflect the exceptional talents of Arabic–Islamic civilization, although the collection remains small in relation to its ambitious setting. Temporary exhibitions are often of a high quality and cover both historical and contemporary themes in arts, crafts and photography. There is an audiovisual complex in the basement with thousands of slides, photographs, films and sound recordings, and current news broadcasts from all over the Arab world are also available for viewing.

HIGHLIGHTS

- Light screens
- Astrolabes in museum
- Sculpted wood and ivory
- Head of sun god
- High-speed transparent elevators
- Sultan Selim III's Koran
- Miniature of Emperor Aurengzeb
- Indian glass vase
- Egyptian child's tunic
- Tapestries

INFORMATION

www.imarabe.org

P9; Locator map F3

1 rue des Fossés Saint-Bernard 75005

01 40 51 38 38; recorded information 01 40 51 38 11

Tue–Sun 10–6

Caféteria at ground level; panoramic rooftop restaurant, Le Ziryab (9th floor)

Jussieu, Cardinal Lemoine

24, 63, 67, 86, 87, 89

Excellent

Museum inexpensive; exhibits expensive

Île Saint-Louis (▶ 46), Arènes de Lutèce (▶ 61)

Occasional Arab music, films and plays

Musée Carnavalet

HIGHLIGHTS

- Statue of Louis XIV
- Le Brun's ceiling painting
- *Destruction of the Bastille,* Hubert Robert
- Bastille prison keys
- Le Sueur's comic-strip
- Proust's bedroom
- Ballroom from Hôtel de Wendel
- Napoleon's picnic-case

INFORMATION

www.paris.fr/musees/
musee_carnavalet

⊞ Q7; Locator map F3

✉ 23 rue de Sévigné 75003

☎ 01 44 59 58 58

🕐 Tue–Sun 10–6

Ⓜ St-Paul

🚌 29, 69, 76, 96

♿ Excellent 🅿 Free; temporary exhibitions moderate

↔ Place des Vosges (➤ 49), Musée Picasso (➤ 53)

There is no better museum than this to plunge you into the history of Paris, and its renovated mansion setting is hard to beat. Period rooms, artefacts, documents and paintings combine to show you the city's turbulent past.

Ornamental excess This captivating collection is displayed within two adjoining 16th- and 17th-century town houses. The main entrance is through the superb courtyard of the Hôtel Carnavalet (1548), once home of the celebrated writer Madame de Sévigné. Here attention focuses on the Roman period, the Middle Ages, the Renaissance and the heights of decorative excess reached under Louis XIV, Louis XV and Louis XVI. Some of the richly painted and sculpted interiors are original to the building; others, such as the wood panelling from the Hôtel Colbert de Villacerf and Brunetti's *trompe-l'œil* staircase paintings, have been brought in.

Revolution to the present Next door, the well-renovated Hôtel Le Peletier de Saint-Fargeau (1690) exhibits some remarkable objects from the Revolution—a period when anything and everything was emblazoned with slogans—and continues with Napoleon I's reign, the Restoration, the Second Empire, the Commune and finally the belle-époque. Illustrious figures such as Robespierre and Madame de Récamier come to life within their chronological context. The collection ends in the early 20th century with some remarkable reconstructions of interiors, and paintings by Maurice Utrillo, Paul Signac, Albert Marquet and Leónard Foujita.

Place des Vosges

Paris's best-preserved square connects the quarters of the Marais and the Bastille. You can marvel at its architectural unity and stroll under its arcades, now animated by outdoor restaurants and window-shoppers.

Place Royale Ever since the square was inaugurated in 1612 with a spectacular fireworks display, countless luminaries have chosen to live in the red-brick houses overlooking the central garden of plane trees. Before that, the square was the site of a royal palace, the Hôtel des Tournelles (1407), that was later abandoned and demolished by Catherine de Médicis in 1559 when her husband Henri II died in a tournament. The arcaded façades were commissioned by the enlightened Henri IV, who incorporated two royal pavilions at the centre of the north and south sides of the square and named it Place Royale.

Celebrities After the Revolution the square was renamed place des Vosges in honour of the first French district to pay its new taxes. The first example of planned development in the history of Paris, these 36 town houses (nine on each side and still intact after four centuries) with their steep-pitched roofs surround a formal garden laid out with gravel paths and fountains. The elegant symmetry of the houses has always attracted a string of celebrities including princesses, official mistresses, Cardinal Richelieu, the Duc de Sully, Victor Hugo (his house is now a museum) and Théophile Gautier. More recently the late painter Francis Bacon, Beaubourg's architect Richard Rogers and former minister of culture, Jack Lang, have all lived here. Upmarket shops and chic art galleries, with prices to match and ideal for window-shopping, line its arcades.

HIGHLIGHTS

- Pavillon du Roi
- Pavillon de la Reine
- Statue of Louis XIII
- No. 6, Maison de Victor Hugo
- No. 21, residence of Cardinal Richelieu
- Door knockers
- *Trompe-l'œil* bricks
- Auvergne sausages at Ma Bourgogne restaurant

INFORMATION

www.paris.fr/musees/ maison_de_victor_hugo

- Q7–Q8; Locator map F3
- place des Vosges 75004
- Ma Bourgogne (► 71)
- Bastille, Chemin Vert, St-Paul
- 29, 69, 76, 96
- Good
- Free
- Hôtel de Sully (► 23), Musée Carnavalet (► 48)

Cimetière du Père Lachaise

INFORMATION

www.paris.org
- Off map; Locator map off F2
- boulevard de Ménilmontant 75020
- 01 55 25 82 10
- Mid-Mar to early Nov Mon–Fri 8–6, Sat 8.30–6, Sun 9–6; Nov–mid-Mar Mon–Fri 8–5.30, Sat 8.30–5.30, Sun 9–5.30
- Père Lachaise
- 61, 69
- Good; hilly terrain, but individual cars admitted
- Free; guided tours inexpensive
- Guided tours (in English Jun–Sep)

If you think cemeteries are lugubrious then a visit to Père Lachaise may change your mind. A plethora of tomb designs, shady trees and twisting paths combine to create a peaceful setting that is also a popular park.

Pilgrimage This landscaped hillside, up in the *faubourgs* of Ménilmontant, is now a popular haunt for rock fans, Piaf fans and lovers of poetry, literature, music and history. Since its creation in 1803 this vast cemetery has seen hundreds of the famous and illustrious buried within its precincts, so that a walk around its labyrinthine expanse presents a microcosm of French sociocultural history. Pick up a plan at the entrance or buy one from a neighbouring shop, then set off on this Parisian path of the Holy Grail to track down your heroes.

Incumbents The cemetery was created in 1803 on land once owned by Louis XIV's confessor, Father La Chaise. It was the site of the Communards' tragic last stand in 1871, when the 147 survivors of a nightlong fight met their bloody end in front of a government firing-squad and were thrown into a communal grave, now commemorated by the Mur des Fédérés in the eastern corner. A sombre reminder of the victims of World War II are the memorials to those who died in the Nazi concentration camps. Paths meander past striking funerary monuments and the graves of such well-known figures as the star-crossed medieval lovers Abélard and Héloïse, painters Delacroix and Modigliani, actress Sarah Bernhardt, composers Poulenc and Bizet, and writers Balzac and Colette. Crowds of rock fans throng round the tomb of Jim Morrison, singer with The Doors, whose death in Paris in 1971 is still a mystery.

PARIS's
best

51

Museums & Galleries

OTHER MUSEUMS

If you are hooked on the intimate atmosphere of one-man museums, then head for the former home/studio of sculptor Antoine Bourdelle, renovated in 1992 by top architect Christian de Portzamparc (✉ 18 rue Antoine-Bourdelle 75015 🚇 Falguière). Other jewels include the Maison de Victor Hugo (➤ 49), the Musée Delacroix (➤ 62), the Musée Hébert (➤ 62), the Maison de Balzac (47 rue Raynouard 75016 🚇 Passy) and the Musée Gustave Moreau (14 rue de la Rochefoucauld 75009 🚇 Trinité).

Visit the Musée d'Art Moderne for modern and contemporary paintings and sculpture

CITÉ DES SCIENCES ET DE L'INDUSTRIE

Vast, enthralling display covering the Earth, the universe, life, communications, natural resources, technology and industry. There are temporary exhibitions, a planetarium, an aquarium, a submarine, a children's section and a hemispherical screen cinema, La Géode (➤ 60).

➕ Off map at Q1 ✉ 30 avenue Corentin Cariou 75019 ☎ 01 40 05 80 00; www.cite-sciences.fr 🕐 Tue–Sat 10–6, Sun 10–7 🍽 Cafés in park 🚇 Porte de la Villette 💰 Expensive

MAISON EUROPÉENNE DE LA PHOTOGRAPHIE

Stylish complex for contemporary photography, which stages dynamic temporary shows.

➕ P8 ✉ 5–7 rue de Fourcy 75004 ☎ 01 44 78 75 00; www.mep-fr.org 🕐 Wed–Sun 11am–8am 🚇 St-Paul 💰 Moderate

MUSÉE D'ART MODERNE DE LA VILLE DE PARIS

Dufy's mural *La Fée Electricité*, Matisse's *La Danse* and a solid collection of the early moderns. Restoration work due to last until the end of 2005.

➕ C5 ✉ 11 avenue du Président-Wilson 75116 ☎ Information 01 53 67 40 00 🍽 Café 🚇 Iéna, Alma-Marceau 💰 Inexpensive

MUSÉE DES ARTS ET MÉTIERS

An eccentric museum where art meets science through antique clocks, optics, underwater items including a diving suite, vintage cars and mechanical toys.

➕ N5–P5 ✉ 60 rue Réaumur 75003 ☎ 01 53 01 82 00; www.arts-et-metiers.net

🕐 Tue–Sun 10–6 (also Thu until 9.30pm) 🚇 Arts et Métiers, Réaumur-Sébastopol 💷 Moderate

MUSÉE D'ART ET D'HISTOIRE DU JUDAÏSME

Jewish art and culture from medieval times to the present day, concentrating mainly on France but also including the rest of Europe and North Africa. Exhibits range from wedding items to works by Jewish artists such as Modigliani and Chagall.

➕ P6 ✉ Hôtel de Saint-Aignan, 71 rue du Temple 75003 ☎ 01 53 01 86 60; www.mahj.org 🕐 Mon–Fri 11–6, Sun 10–6 🚇 Rambuteau, Hotel de Ville 💷 Moderate

MUSÉE JACQUEMART-ANDRÉ

An elegant mansion hosts this fine collection of around 150 paintings, including works by Canaletto, Rembrandt, Bellini and Van Dyck.

➕ E2 ✉ 158 boulevard Haussmann 75008 ☎ 01 45 62 11 59; www.musee-jacquemart-andre.com 🕐 Daily 10–6 🚇 St-Philippe-du-Roule, Miromesnil 💷 Expensive

MUSÉE NATIONAL DES ARTS ASIATIQUES–GUIMET

One of the world's leading museums of Asian art, the Musée Guimet has the finest collection of Khmer (Cambodian) art in the West.

➕ B5 ✉ 6 place d'Iéna 75116 ☎ 01 56 52 53 00; www.museeguimet.fr 🕐 Wed–Mon 10–6 🚇 Iéna 💷 Inexpensive

MUSÉUM NATIONAL D'HISTOIRE NATURELLE

Spectacular displays of comparative anatomy, paleontology and mineralogy. Interesting temporary exhibitions and botanical gardens dating from the 17th century.

➕ P11 ✉ 57 rue Cuvier 75005 ☎ 01 40 79 30 00; www.mnhn.fr 🕐 Grande Galerie de l'Evolution Wed–Mon 10–6. Paleontology and Mineralogy Wed–Mon 10–5 🚇 Place Monge, Gare d'Austerlitz 💷 Prices vary for individual galleries

MUSÉE PICASSO

Massive collection of Picasso's paintings, sculptures, drawings and ceramics in a beautifully renovated 17th-century mansion. The fixtures are by Diego Giacometti, and some of the works are by Picasso's contemporaries.

➕ Q6 ✉ Hôtel Salé, 5 rue de Thorigny 75003 ☎ 01 42 71 25 21; www.musee-picasso.fr 🕐 Wed–Mon 9.30–5.30 (also until 6, Apr–Sep) 🚇 St-Paul 🚌 29 💷 Inexpensive

Grand Nu au Fauteuil Rouge, *in the Musée Picasso*

COMING SOON

A new museum is set to open in 2006, dedicated to non-European art. Provisionally called the Musée du Quai Branly (Arts et Civilisations d'Afrique, d'Asie, d'Océanie et des Amériques), the museum will be sited at quai Branly, near the Eiffel Tower (www.quaibranly.fr).

MUSÉE PICASSO

The contents of the Musée Picasso—including 251 paintings, 160 sculptures and 1, 500 drawings—were acquired by France in lieu of inheritance tax. The process of evaluating Picasso's vast estate was no simple task as he had the annoying habit of leaving a château once the rooms were filled with his prodigious works. Legal wrangling with his heirs finally produced this superb selection, one quarter of his collection.

53

Places of Worship

Saint-Étienne-du-Mont

ÉGLISE SAINT-ÉTIENNE-DU-MONT

Dating from the 15th century, a bizarre combination of Gothic, Renaissance and classical architecture. Unique wood screen arching over the nave.

🕂 M10 ⊠ place Sainte-Genevieve 75005 🚇 Cardinal Lemoine

ÉGLISE SAINT-EUSTACHE

Renaissance in detail and decoration but medieval in general design. Frequent organ recitals.

🕂 M5 ⊠ rue Rambuteau 75001 🚇 Les Halles

ÉGLISE SAINT-GERMAIN-DES-PRÉS

Paris's oldest abbey dates from the 11th century; it preserves 12th-century flying buttresses, an original tower and the choir. Regular organ recitals.

🕂 K8 ⊠ place Saint-Germain-des-Prés 75006
🚇 St-Germain-des-Prés

ÉGLISE SAINT-MERRI

Superb example of Flamboyant Gothic though not completed until 1612. Renaissance stained glass, murals, impressive organ loft and Paris's oldest church bell (1331). Concerts are held regularly.

🕂 N6/7 ⊠ 78 rue Saint-Martin 75004 ☎ 01 42 71 40 75 for concert information 🚇 Hôtel de Ville

ÉGLISE SAINT-SÉVERIN

Rebuilt from the 13th to the 16th centuries on the site of a 12th-century oratory. Inside is an impressive double ambulatory, palm-tree vaulting and the Chapelle Mansart. Lovely stained-glass windows.

🕂 M8 ⊠ 1 rue des Prêtres Saint-Séverin 75005 🚇 St-Michel

ÉGLISE SAINT-SULPICE

Construction started in 1646 and ended 134 years later, producing asymmetrical towers and very mixed styles. Note Delacroix's murals in the first chapel on the right, the famous organs and statues by Jacques-Edme Dumont.

🕂 K9 ⊠ place Saint-Sulpice 75006 🕐 7.30–7.30
🚇 St-Sulpice

LA MOSQUÉE

This startling Moorish construction (1926) has a richly decorated interior, patio and arcaded garden. Relax in the hammam (see panel ➤ 83) or sip mint tea.

🕂 N11 ⊠ place du Puits-de-l'Ermite 75005 ☎ 01 45 35 97 33 🕐 Guided tours Sat–Thu 9–noon, 2–6 🍴 Tea room 🚇 Jussieu/Place Monge 💷 Inexpensive

---

SAINT-GERMAIN-DES-PRÉS

The first church of Saint-Germain-des-Prés was erected in the 6th century in the middle of fields (*les prés*). From the 8th century the church was part of a Benedictine abbey but was destroyed by the Normans, after which the present church was built. The monastery was surrounded by a fortified wall and adjoined a bishop's palace, but this eventually made way for housing in the late 17th century.

Cult Cafés & Salons de Thé

LES DEUX MAGOTS
Some 25 whisky brands, a good mix of tourists and the literary shades of Simone de Beauvoir, Truman Capote and Hemingway. Strategic spot for street artists.
🕂 J8 ✉ 170 boulevard Saint-Germain 75006 ☎ 01 45 48 55 25 🕙 Daily 7.30am–1.30am 🚇 St-Germain-des-Prés

Les Deux Magots, in boulevard Saint-Germain

CAFÉ BEAUBOURG
Opposite the Pompidou Centre, a favourite with artists, critics and book-reading poseurs. Discreet tables in spacious setting designed by Christian de Portzamparc.
🕂 N6 ✉ 43 rue Saint-Merri 75004 ☎ 01 48 87 63 96 🕙 Sun–Wed 8am–1am, Thu–Sat 8am–2am 🚇 Hôtel de Ville, Chatelet, Rambuteau

LA CLOSERIE DES LILAS
Hot spot of history's makers and shakers, including Lenin, Trotsky, Paul Verlaine and James Joyce.
🕂 Off map at K11 ✉ 171 boulevard du Montparnasse 75006 ☎ 01 40 51 34 50 🕙 Daily 11am–2am 🚇 Vavin, Raspail

CAFÉ DE FLORE
Haunted by ghosts of existentialists Sartre and de Beauvoir, who held court here during the Occupation. Wildly overpriced but great for people-watching.
🕂 J8 ✉ 172 boulevard Saint-Germain 75006 ☎ 01 45 48 55 26 🕙 Daily 7.30am–1.30am 🚇 St-Germain-des-Prés

CAFÉ MARLY
A fashionable watering hole where elegance is assured by the setting overlooking the Louvre pyramid, and by the intelligent decoration.
🕂 K6 ✉ cour Napoléon, 93 rue de Rivoli 75001 ☎ 01 49 26 06 60 🕙 Daily 8am–2am 🚇 Palais-Royal, Musée du Louvre

AUX DÉLICES DE SCOTT
This elegant café with fine cakes and pastries was once frequented by Clemenceau and Sarah Bernhardt.
🕂 Off map at E1 ✉ 39 avenue de Villiers 75017 ☎ 01 47 63 71 36 🕙 Mon–Fri 8.45am–6.30pm, Sat noon–6 🚇 Malesherbes

MARIAGE FRÈRES
Chic and expensive tea room upstairs. Over 460 teas from 20 countries.
🕂 L8 ✉ 13 rue des Grands-Augustins 75006 ☎ 01 40 51 82 50 🕙 Daily noon–7 🚇 Odéon

THE CROISSANT

As you sit over your morning *café au lait* eating a croissant, meditate on the origins of this quintessential French product. It was invented when Vienna was besieged by the Turks in 1683. A baker heard underground noises and informed the authorities, who found the enemy tunnelling away into the city. The baker's reward was permission to produce pastries—so he created one in the form of the Islamic crescent.

55

20th-Century Architecture

GRANDS PROJETS

President Mitterrand was responsible for many of Paris's late-20th-century monuments. For over a decade cranes groaned as the state's *grands projets* emerged from their foundations. Intellectual criteria often came before functional considerations, and consequently not all monuments operate successfully. The Louvre renovation, topped by I. M. Pei's pyramid, is a notable exception.

BIBLIOTHÈQUE NATIONALE DE FRANCE

Mitterrand's last pet *grand projet.* Dominique Perrault's symbolic design was dogged by technical and functional problems until it finally opened in early 1997.
🚇 Off map at Q11　✉ 11 quai François-Mauriac　☎ 01 53 79 59 59; www.bnf.fr　🕐 Tue–Sat 10–8, Sun noon–7　🚇 Quai de la Gare

CITÉ DE LA MUSIQUE

Finally completed in 1995 after 16 years of delays and political volte-face, with a monumental design in white stone by Christian de Portzamparc. Houses a music school, concert hall and museum of music.
🚇 Off map at Q1　✉ 221 avenue Jean-Jaurès 75019　☎ Museum 01 44 84 44 84; www.cite-musique.fr　🕐 Tue–Sat noon–6, Sun 10–6
🍴 Café　🚇 Porte de Pantin　💶 Moderate

LA GRANDE ARCHE

A marble window on the world designed by Otto Von Spreckelsen and completed for the 1989 Bicentennial. Take the exterior elevator for views along the city's historical La Défense–Arc de Triomphe–Louvre axis.
🚇 Off map at A1　✉ 1 Parvis de La Défense　☎ 01 49 07 27 57; www.grandearche.com　🕐 Daily 10–7 (also until 8pm, Apr–Sep); ticket office closes 30 minutes earlier　🚇 La Défense　💶 Moderate

The Grande Arche at La Défense

MAISON DU VERRE

Designed in art-deco style by Pierre Chareau in 1932. Astonishing use of glass.
🚇 H8　✉ 31 rue Saint-Guillaume 75006　🚇 Rue du Bac

NO. 26 RUE VAVIN

This striking, innovative building—designed by Henri Sauvage in 1912—is faced in blue and white ceramic and has stepped balconies.
🚇 J11　✉ 26 rue Vavin 75006　🚇 Vavin

PORTE DAUPHINE

The best remaining example (1902) of Hector Guimard's art-nouveau Métro entrances, with a glass canopy and writhing sculptural structures.
🚇 Off map at A5　✉ avenue Bugeaud 75016　🚇 Porte Dauphine

RUE MALLET-STEVENS

This tiny cul-de-sac houses major symbols of cubist architecture (1927) by Robert Mallet-Stevens. The stark, purist lines and volumes continue at Le Corbusier's nearby Villa Laroche (1923), which is now a foundation.
🚇 Off map at A5　✉ rue Mallet-Stevens, off rue du Dr-Blanche 75016
🚇 Jasmin

Bridges

PONT ALEXANDRE III
Paris's most ornate bridge, rich in gilded cupids and elaborate lamps. Built for the 1900 Exposition Universelle, and dedicated to the Franco-Russian alliance of 1892—the foundation stone was laid in 1896 by Tsar Nicolas II, Tsar Alexander III's son.
✚ F5 🚇 Invalides

PONT DE L'ALMA
Originally built in 1856 to commemorate victory over the Russians in the Crimean War. Replaced in 1974, it crosses the road tunnel in which Princess Diana was killed in 1997—now a place of pilgrimage.
✚ C5 🚇 Alma-Marceau

PONT DES ARTS
The pedestrian bridge of 1804 was replaced in 1985 by an iron structure of seven steel arches crossed by resonant wooden planks. It's a favourite spot for impromptu parties and street performances.
✚ K7 🚇 Louvre-Rivoli

PONT DE BIR-HAKEIM
Paris's double-decker bridge (1903–05) is best experienced by rattling over it in a Métro. Designed by Formigé, with steel columns in art-nouveau style.
✚ A7 🚇 Bir-Hakeim, Passy

PONT MARIE
Named after the Île Saint-Louis property developer, first built in 1635. Once lined with four-storey houses—some later partly destroyed by floods and others demolished in 1788. Rebuilt in 1850.
✚ P8 🚇 Pont Marie

PONT NEUF
Built from 1578 to 1604, Paris's oldest bridge ironically bears the name of 'New Bridge'. The innovative, houseless design was highly controversial at the time. In 1985 it was 'wrapped' by site-artist Christo.
✚ L7 🚇 Pont Neuf

PONT ROYAL
Five classical arches join the Tuileries with the Faubourg Saint-Germain area. Built in 1689 by Gabriel to Mansart's design, it was once used for major Parisian festivities and fireworks.
✚ J6 🚇 Palais-Royal, Musée du Louvre

37 BRIDGES
The Paris motto *'Fluctuat nec mergitur'* (It is buffeted by the waves but it never sinks) did not always hold true. For centuries there were only two bridges, which linked the Île de la Cité north and south. Subsequent wooden bridges sank without trace after floods, fires or riverboat collisions, so the construction of the stone Pont Neuf marked a real advance. The new metal-arched Passerelle de Solferino suspension bridge, which joins the Louvre area and the Musée d'Orsay via the Tuileries Gardens, was inaugurated in 1999. It is the city's 37th bridge.

Pont Alexandre III

57

Green Spaces

Parc Monceau

For information about parks and gardens in Paris
☎ 01 40 71 74 72

PARC DE BAGATELLE

On the west side of the Bois de Boulogne is the Parc de Bagatelle. Its mini-château, built in 1775, was sold in 1870 to Englishman Richard Wallace who added further pavilions and terraces. About 700 varieties of roses bloom here. Nice open-air restaurant (see panel ➤ 64).
◷ Sat–Sun 9–7 (until 8 in summer) 🖐 Inexpensive

JARDIN DES SERRES D'AUTEUIL

Off the tourist beat, and with striking late 19th century tropical greenhouses. The terrace wall is adorned with sculpted masks from Rodin's studio.
➕ Off map at A7 ✉ 3 avenue de la Porte d'Auteuil 17607 ☎ 01 40 71 74 00
◷ Daily 10–5 (until 6 in summer) 🚇 Porte d'Auteuil
🖐 Inexpensive

BOIS DE BOULOGNE

An area of 845ha (2,090 acres), 22km (14 miles) of paths, 56km (35 miles) of roads, 150,000 trees and 300,000 bushes. Distractions from boating to clay-pigeon shooting and gastronomy.
➕ Off map at A5 ◷ Permanently open 🍽 Cafés, restaurants
🚇 Porte Dauphine, Porte d'Auteuil

JARDIN DES TUILERIES

Laid out in 1564, later radically formalized by Le Nôtre. Now replanted to match adjoining Louvre. Maillol's statues rest in the shade of chestnut trees.
➕ H5 ✉ place de la Concorde 75001 ◷ Apr–end Sep daily 7.30am–9pm, Oct–end Mar 7.30–7.30 🍽 Cafés 🚇 Tuileries 🖐 Free

PARC ANDRÉ-CITROËN

A cool futurist 1980s park divided into specialist gardens, on the site of a former Citroën factory.
➕ Off map at A11 ✉ rue Balard, rue Leblanc 75015 ☎ 01 45 58 35 40 ◷ Mon–Fri 8–dusk, Sat,–Sun 9–dusk 🚇 Balard 🖐 Free

PARC MONCEAU

Classic park planted in 1783 by Thomas Blaikie by order of the Duc d'Orléans. Picturesque *faux* ruins.
➕ E1 ✉ boulevard de Courcelles 75008 ☎ 01 42 27 39 56
◷ Apr–end Oct daily 7am–10pm; Nov–end Mar 7am–8pm
🚇 Monceau 🖐 Free

PARC MONTSOURIS

A Haussmann creation designed on English models, with copses, serpentine paths and a small lake.
➕ Off map at K11 ✉ avenue Reille/boulevard Jourdan 75014
◷ Mon–Fri 8–dusk, Sat–Sun 9–dusk 🍽 Restaurant 🚇 RER Line B Cité Universitaire 🖐 Free

Views

ARC DE TRIOMPHE
Situated at the hub of Haussmann's web of 12 avenues, which reach out like tentacles towards the city beyond, and the ultimate symbol of Napoleon's military pretensions and might. It is worth climbing the 284 steps to the terrace for superb panoramic views of the city. Video projections.

B2 place Charles-de-Gaulle 75008 01 55 37 73 77; www.monum.fr Apr–end Sep daily 10am–11pm; Oct–end Mar 10am–10.30pm Charles de Gaulle-Étoile Moderate

LA SAMARITAINE
The 10th floor at Magasin 2 offers a spectacular close-up on the city's Left Bank monuments. Lunch in the open air on the 10th floor or dine in splendour at the 5th-floor restaurant.

L6 rue de la Monnaie 75001 01 40 41 20 20 Mon–Sat 9.30–7 (also Thu until 9, Sat until 8). Rooftop open mid-Mar to mid-Dec Cafeteria, restaurant Pont Neuf Free

SQUARE DU VERT GALANT
Quintessential river-level view of bridges and the Louvre, shaded by willows and stunning at sunset. The square forms the west point of the Île de la Cité.

L7 place du Pont-Neuf 75001 Apr–end Sep daily 9am–10pm; Oct–end Mar 9–5.30 Pont Neuf

TOUR MONTPARNASSE
The 56th-floor viewing gallery and the 59th-floor terrace of this 209-m (685-ft) modern tower in Montparnasse offer breathtaking views of the city. On a clear day you can see up to 40km (25 miles) away. Films on Paris are screened, in French, on the 56th floor.

G11 33 avenue du Maine 75015 01 45 38 52 56; www.tourmontparnasse56.com Apr–end Sep daily 9.30am–11.30pm; Oct–end Mar 9.30am–10.30pm Bar, restaurant Montparnasse-Bienvenüe Moderate

POLLUTION OVER PARIS

The promised views over Paris do not always materialize as the capital is often hidden in haze trapped by the saucer-like shape of the Île de France. Measures taken since the mid-1970s have helped: In one decade industrial pollution was reduced by 50 per cent and the replacement of coal by nuclear energy and gas further cleared the air. However, carbon-monoxide levels (from vehicle exhausts) can still exceed European Union norms.

The view from Tour Montparnasse

For Children

LE GUIGNOL

A juvenile crowd-puller dating back to the early 19th century is the *guignol*, an open-air puppet show held in several Parisian parks. You'll find them in summer on Wednesdays, weekends and during school holidays at parks such as the Luxembourg, Montsouris, Buttes Chaumont, Champ de Mars and the Jardin d'Acclimatation.

DISNEYLAND PARIS
This popular resort is adding new attractions all the time, including the Walt Disney Studio park.
➕ Off map to east ✉ 77777 Marne-la-Vallée ☎ Recorded information 01 60 30 60 30; www.disneylandparis.com 🕐 Mon–Fri 10–8, Sat–Sun 9–8 (late nights in summer; enquire) 🍴 Cafés, restaurants 🚇 RER Line A Marne-la-Vallée-Chessy 💰 Expensive

LA GÉODE
The hemispherical screen plunges viewers into the heart of the action with frequent showings of nature and science films. Near by are Le Cinaxe, a simulator cinema and the Cité des Sciences et de l'Industrie (➤ 52), with other children's activities.
➕ Off map at Q1 ✉ 26 avenue Corentin Cariou 75019 ☎ 01 39 17 10 00; www.Lageode.fr 🕐 Tue–Sat 10.30–9.30, Sun 10.30–7 (film times vary) 🍴 Cafés in park 🚇 Porte de la Villette 💰 Moderate

GRÉVIN
Mingle with the celebrities of today and Parisians of a bygone time at this waxwork museum.
➕ L3 ✉ 10 Boulevard Montmartre 75009 ☎ 01 47 70 85 05; www.grevin.com 🕐 Mon–Fri 10–6.30, Sat–Sun 10–7 🍴 Cafés, restaurants 🚇 Grand Boulevards 💰 Expensive

JARDIN D'ACCLIMATATION
A specially designed section of the Bois de Boulogne with puppet theatre, playground, fairground, educational museum, circus, zoo and minitrain.
➕ Off map ✉ Main entrance boulevard des Sablons ☎ 01 40 67 90 82; www.jardindacclimatation.fr 🕐 Jun–end Sep daily 10–7; Oct–end May 10–6 🍴 Café 🚇 Les Sablons 💰 Inexpensive

PARC ASTÉRIX
Some 35km (22 miles) north of Paris, this very Gallic theme park is dedicated to the comic-strip hero Astérix. Animation, rides, games.
➕ Off map to north ✉ 60128 Plailly ☎ 03 44 62 31 31, reservations 08 26 30 10 40; ww.parcasterix.fr 🕐 Days and times vary, call ahead; closed in winter 🍴 Cafés, restaurants 🚇 RER Line B, Roissy-Charles de Gaulle, then bus every 30 minutes 💰 Expensive

La Géode

What's Free

ARÈNES DE LUTÈCE
A partly ruined Gallo-Roman amphitheatre now popular with *boules*-playing retirees and teenagers. Destroyed in AD280, it was restored in the early 1900s.

➕ N10 ✉ rue des Arènes/47 rue Monge 75005 🕐 Apr–end Sep daily 9am–9.30pm; Oct–end Mar 8–5.30 🚇 Jussieu, Cardinal Lemoine

DROUOT RICHELIEU
Let yourself be tempted at Paris's main auction rooms. A Persian carpet, a Louis XV commode or a bunch of cutlery may come under the hammer.

➕ L2 ✉ 9 rue Drouot 75009 ☎ 01 48 00 20 20; www.drouot.fr 🕐 Mon–Sat 11–6 (auctions start at 2pm); closed Aug 🚇 Richelieu-Drouot

JARDIN DU PALAIS-ROYAL
Elegant 18th-century arcades surround this peaceful formal garden and palace (now the Conseil d'État and the Ministère de la Culture), redolent of Revolutionary history. Daniel Buren's conceptual striped columns (1986) occupy the Cour d'Honneur.

➕ K5 ✉ place du Palais-Royal 75001 🕐 Daily 7.30am–8.30pm (closing time varies with the season) 🍴 Restaurants 🚇 Palais-Royal, Musée du Louvre

MÉMORIAL DE LA DÉPORTATION
In the Île de la Cité's eastern tip is a starkly designed crypt lined with 200,000 quartz pebbles to commemorate French citizens deported by the Nazis.

➕ N8 ✉ square de l'Île de France 75004 🕐 Mon–Fri 8.30–5.30, Sat–Sun 9–5.30 🚇 Cité

MUSÉE COGNACQ-JAY
This charming museum displays the 18th-century paintings and objets d'art collected by Ernest Cognacq and his wife Louise Jay, founders of the department store La Samaritaine. It is set in a mansion furnished in 18th-century style.

➕ Q7 ✉ Hôtel Donon, 8 rue Elzévir 75003 ☎ 01 40 27 07 🕐 Tue–Sun 10–6 🚇 St-Paul

PAVILLON DE L'ARSENAL
This strikingly designed building houses well-conceived exhibitions on urban Paris alongside a permanent display of the city's architectural evolution.

➕ Q9 ✉ 21 boulevard Morland 75004 ☎ 01 42 76 33 97

BARGAIN PARIS

Nothing comes cheap in this city of light. Still, although gastronomy, official culture and history cost money, browsing at the *bouquinistes* along the Seine, picnicking on the river banks, reading in the parks, exploring back streets and spinning hours away for the cost of a coffee on a *terrasse* are some of Paris's bargains.

The Palais Royal

61

Intriguing Streets

BOULEVARD DE ROCHECHOUART

Teeming with struggling immigrants. Impromptu markets, cheap clothing, jewellery and seedy sex shops, and a pervasive aroma of *merguez* and fries.
✚ Off map ☺ Barbès-Rochechouart

COUR DU COMMERCE-SAINT-ANDRÉ

A narrow cobbled passage tucked away on the Left Bank, the Cour du Commerce-Saint-André connects rue Saint-André-des-Arts with boulevard Saint-Germain and dates from 1776, though it incorporates a medieval tower. It became a hive of Revolutionary activity, with Marat printing pamphlets at No. 8, Danton installed at No. 20 and the anatomy professor Dr. Guillotin (inventor of that 'philanthropic beheading machine') at No. 9.

RUE DU CHERCHE-MIDI

César's sculpture on the rue de Sèvres crossroads marks out this typical Left Bank street, home to the famous Poîlane bakery (No. 8) and the Musée Hébert (No. 85). Main interest ends at the Boulevard Raspail.
✚ G10–J9 ☺ St-Sulpice

RUE DU FAUBOURG SAINT-HONORÉ

Price tags and politics cohabit in this street of luxury. See Hermès' imaginative window dressing or salute the gendarmes in front of the Élysée Palace.
✚ C1–G4 ☺ Madeleine/Miromesnil

RUE JACOB

Antique and interior-decoration shops monopolize this picturesque stretch. Make a 20-pace detour to the Musée Delacroix on the delightful rue de Furstemberg.
✚ J7–K8 ☺ St-Germain-des-Prés

RUE MONSIEUR-LE-PRINCE

An uphill stretch lined with university bookshops, antique and ethnic shops and a sprinkling of student restaurants. Sections of the medieval city wall are embedded in Nos. 41 and 47.
✚ L9 ☺ Odéon

RUE DES ROSIERS

Effervescent street at the heart of Paris's Jewish quarter. Kosher butchers and restaurants and Hebrew bookshops rub shoulders with designer boutiques. Quietens considerably on Saturdays.
✚ P7 ☺ St-Paul

Shopfront on the rue des Rosiers

RUE VIEILLE-DU-TEMPLE

The pulse of the hip Marais district, dense in bars, cafés, boutiques and, farther north, the historic Hôtel Amelot-de-Bisseuil (No. 47), the Maison J. Hérouët, the Hôtel de Rohan (No. 87) and the garden of the Musée Picasso (➤ 53).
✚ P7–Q6 ☺ St-Paul

PARIS
where to

Elegant Restaurants

PRICES

Prices are approximate, based on a 3-course meal for one person

€€€   over €80
€€   €20–€80
€   under €20

ROSE-TINTED DINING

Le Pré Catelan (€€€) has an elegant setting near the rose gardens of the Parc de Bagatelle, and both indoor and outdoor seating. Precise, sophisticated modern cooking and exquisite desserts.
➕ A2 ✉ Bois de Boulogne, Route de Suresnes 75016 ☎ 01 44 14 14 14 🕐 Closed Sun, Mon

6 NEW YORK (€€)

A recent addition to the Paris restaurant scene, New York offers beautiful contemporary decor and fusion food.
➕ C5 ✉ 6 avenue de New York 75016 (Champs Élysées) ☎ 01 40 70 03 30 🕐 Closed Sat lunch, Sun 🚇 Alma-Marceau

LE CÉLADON (€€€)

Chef Christophe Moisand's cuisine offers interesting variations on some French classics, including green asparagus in a nutty sauce and roast figs with honey ice cream.
➕ J3 ✉ 15 rue Daunou 75002 (Opéra) ☎ 01 47 03 40 42 🕐 Closed Sat, Sun 🚇 Opéra

LE CIEL DE PARIS (€€)

Enjoy stunning views as you eat in Europe's highest restaurant. Try the lobster and wild mushrooms in red-wine sauce.
➕ G11 ✉ 33 avenue du Maine 75015 (Montparnasse) ☎ 01 40 64 77 64 🕐 Daily 🚇 Montparnasse Bienvenüe

GEORGES (€€)

Slick and sleek, Georges has become one of the fashionable sites for a meal, albeit the dazzling view of Paris from atop the Centre Pompidou and the restaurant's stunning terrace can outshine the nouvelle cuisine.
➕ N6 ✉ Centre Pompidou 6th floor, rue Rambuteau 75004 (Les Halles) ☎ 01 44 78 47 99 🕐 Mon, Wed–Sun noon–1am 🚇 Rambuteau

GUY SAVOY (€€€)

One of the city's gastronomic temples where Guy Savoy makes cooking an art form.
➕ B2 ✉ 18 rue Troyon 75017 (Champs Élysées) ☎ 01 43 80 40 61 🕐 Closed Sat lunch, Sun, Mon 🚇 Charles de Gaulle-Etoile

JACQUES CAGNA (€€€)

Chef Jacques Cagan has been reinventing French classics for more than 30 years. Expect true delacies in an elegant, townhouse setting.
➕ L8 ✉ 14 rue des Grands-Augustins 75006 (Saint-Germain-des-Près) ☎ 01 43 26 49 39 🕐 Closed Mon, Sat lunch, Sun 🚇 St-Michel, Odéon

SPOON (€€€)

Trendy bistro-style restaurant with open kitchen and changing décor; famous chef Alain Ducasse's highly original 'world food' menu attracts all manner of gourmets.
➕ D4 ✉ 14 rue de Marignan 75008 (Champs Élysées) ☎ 01 40 76 34 44 🕐 Closed Sat lunch, Sun 🚇 Franklin D. Roosevelt

TAILLEVENT (€€€)

Discreetly elegant restaurant with candelabras and wood panelling. The cooking has solid, classical foundations, with subtle contemporary leanings.
➕ D2 ✉ 15 rue Lamennais 75008 (Champs Élysées) ☎ 01 44 95 15 01 🕐 Closed Sat, Sun, Aug 🚇 George V

LA TOUR D'ARGENT (€€€)

Historic restaurant best known for duck. Fabulous view, and great wine cellar.
➕ N9 ✉ 15–17 quai de la Tournelle 75005 (facing Île Saint-Louis) ☎ 01 43 54 23 31 🕐 Closed Tue lunch, Mon 🚇 Pont-Marie, Cardinal Lemoine

Regional French Restaurants

L'ALIVI (€€)
Picturesque restaurant devoted to Corsican cuisine (fresh sardines with fennel, pigeon stuffed with figs) served with local wines.
➕ P7 ✉ 27 rue du Rou de Sicile 75004 (Marais) ☎ 01 48 87 90 20 ⏰ Daily 🚇 St-Paul

L'ALSACE (€€)
A little piece of eastern France in the heart of Paris. Brasserie-style cuisine, including seafood platters, sauerkraut and apple strudel. Summer terrace.
➕ D3 ✉ 39 avenue des Champs Élysées 75008 (Champs Élysées) ☎ 01 53 93 97 00 ⏰ Daily 🚇 Franklin D. Roosevelt

L'AMBASSADE D'AUVERGNE (€€)
Rustic decor and authentic, robust farmhouse cooking from the mountainous Auvergne region. Wines from central France .
➕ N6 ✉ 22 rue du Grenier Saint-Lazare 75003 (Marais/Beaubourg) ☎ 01 42 72 31 22 ⏰ Daily 🚇 Rambuteau

L'AMI JEAN (€€)
Unassuming, friendly restaurant specializing in dishes from the Basque region, near the Spanish border. Veal, beef and seafood enhanced by fine wines.
➕ D6 ✉ 27 rue Malar 75007 (Invalides) ☎ 01 47 05 86 89 ⏰ Closed Sun, Mon 🚇 Invalides, Pont de l'Alma

L'AUBERGE DU MOUTON BLANC (€€)
Once frequented by Molière and Racine, this restaurant now offers traditional regional cuisine such as leg of lamb and steak tartare.
➕ Off map at A10 ✉ 40 rue d'Auteuil 75016 (Auteuil) ☎ 01 42 88 02 21 ⏰ Daily 🚇 Michel-Ange Auteuil

LA BARACANE (€€)
Tiny, tastefully decorated bistro whose menu homes in on Gascony, cassoulet and duck.
➕ Off map at Q7 ✉ 38 rue des Tournelles 75004 (Bastille) ☎ 01 42 71 43 33 ⏰ Closed Sat lunch, Sun 🚇 Bastille

BENOIT (€€€)
Long-standing favourite, serving classic regional dishes. Be sure to reserve ahead.
➕ N7 ✉ 20 rue Saint-Martin 75004 (Les Halles) ☎ 01 42 72 25 76 ⏰ Daily 🚇 Châtelet

BRASSERIE FLO (€€)
A little further out is the characterful Alsatian brasserie that dishes up mountains of delicious *choucroute spéciale*. This restaurant is always noisy, popular and chaotic.
➕ N3 ✉ 7 cour des Petites Ecuries 75010 (Gare de l'Est) ☎ 01 47 70 13 59 ⏰ Daily until 1.30am 🚇 Château d'Eau

CARRÉ DES FEUILLANTS (€€€)
Elegant setting for Alain Dutournier's brilliant evocation of the cooking of his beloved native Gascony. He uses the best-possible ingredients to marvellous effect.
➕ J5 ✉ 14 rue de Castiglione 75001 (Louvre/Palais Royal) ☎ 01 42 86 82 82 ⏰ Closed Sat, Sun, Aug 🚇 Tuileries

FRENCH MEAN CUISINE

'The only cooks in the civilized world are French. Other races have different interpretations of food. Only the French mean *cuisine* because their qualities—rapidity, decision-making, tact—are used. Who has ever seen a foreigner succeed in making a white sauce?'
–Nestor Roqueplan (1804–70), Editor of *Le Figaro*.

ALSACE AND THE SOUTHWEST

Gastronomically speaking, Alsace and the southwest are probably the best-represented regions in Paris. Numerous brasseries churn out *choucroute* (sauerkraut), but it is the southwest that carries off the prizes with its variations on goose and duck. Recent research has found that inhabitants of this region have unexpectedly low rates of cardiac disease—despite their daily consumption of cholesterol-high *foie gras*.

Brasseries & Bistros

BRASSERIE?

A brasserie is the French for brewery, but nowadays describes a lively, smart, yet informal restaurant that serves food at any time of the day and often late into the night. Beer remains a feature, with some brasseries offering quite an extensive selection. Typical dishes include *choucroute*, a hearty blend of sauerkraut and assorted sausages, *blanquette de veau* (veal in cream sauce) and steak *pommes frites* (fries)—frequently described as the national dish of France. Shellfish plays a major part, as witnessed by the mountainous displays outside many brasseries on Paris's more fashionable boulevards.

OR BISTRO?

A bistro is basically a small, modest, often family-run establishment with a short menu of traditional, home-style cooking, together with a good selection of local cheeses. Wine is offered by the carafe or *pichet* (jug), with only a small selection available by the bottle.

ALLARD (€€)

In this authentic Parisian bistro, tradition is all around you, including the food: roast duck with olives, Bresse chicken, turbot in butter sauce.....
✚ L8 ✉ 41 rue St-André des Arts 7006 (Quartier Latin) ☎ 01 43 26 48 23 🕐 Closed Sun 🚇 St-Michel

BOFINGER (€€)

Claims to be Paris's oldest brasserie (1864). Soaring glass dome, lots of mirrors and chandeliers. Seafood, *choucroute* and steaks.
✚ Off map at Q8 ✉ 5 rue de la Bastille 75004 (Bastille) ☎ 01 42 72 87 82 🕐 Daily 🚇 Bastille

BRASSERIE BALZAR (€€)

Fashionable brasserie near the Sorbonne. Seafood, pigs' trotters, *cassoulet*.
✚ M9 ✉ 49 rue des Ecoles 75005 (Latin Quarter/Saint-Michel) ☎ 01 43 54 13 67 🕐 Daily 🚇 Cluny, La Sorbonne

BRASSERIE LIPP (€€)

Paris's famous brasserie, founded in 1880. Haunt of well-known.
✚ J8 ✉ 151 boulevard Saint-Germain 75006 (Saint-Germain-des-Prés) ☎ 01 45 48 53 91 🕐 Daily 🚇 St-Germain-des-Prés

LE COUDE FOU (€€)

Popular Marais bistro with hearty classics. Excellent wine list.
✚ P7 ✉ 12 rue du Bourg Tibourg 75004 (Marais) ☎ 01 42 77 15 16 🕐 Daily 🚇 Hôtel de Ville

LA COUPOLE (€€)

A Montparnasse institution dating from the 1920s. Wide choice of brasserie food, reasonable late-night menu.
✚ J11 ✉ 102 boulevard du Montparnasse 75014 (Montparnasse) ☎ 01 43 20 14 20 🕐 Daily 8.30am–1am 🚇 Vavin

MARTY (€€)

A 1930s-style brasserie offering deliciously fresh shellfish and other seafood as well as a few good meat dishes.
✚ Off map at N11 ✉ 20 avenue des Gobelins 75005 (Mouffetard) ☎ 01 43 31 39 51 🕐 Daily 🚇 Les Gobelins

AU PETIT RICHE (€€)

Wonderful old 1850s bistro. Reliable traditional cuisine and good Loire wines.
✚ L2 ✉ 25 rue Le Peletier 75009 (Opéra) ☎ 01 47 70 68 68 🕐 Closed Sun 🚇 Richelieu-Drouot

LE PETIT SAINT-BENOÎT (€)

Popular old Saint-Germain classic; decor barely changed since the 1930s. Outside tables in summer.
✚ J7 ✉ 4 rue Saint-Benoît 75006 (Saint-Germain-des-Prés) ☎ 01 42 60 27 92 🕐 Closed Sun 🚇 St-Germain-des-Prés

AU PIED DE COCHON (€€)

Open every day and every night, a convivial brasserie serving classic fare, including their renowned onion soup and pigs' trotters. Touristy but good fun.
✚ L5 ✉ 6 rue Coquillère 75001 (Les Halles) ☎ 01 40 13 77 00 🕐 Daily 24 hours 🚇 Les Halles

Trendy Restaurants

ALCAZAR (€€)
English designer Terence Conran's bar-cum-restaurant offers some of the best fish in town, as well as excellent Sunday brunch. The lounge bar upstairs features international DJs.
🔲 K8 ✉ 62 rue Mazarine 75006 (Saint-Germain-des-Prés) ☎ 01 53 10 19 99 🕐 Daily until 2am 🚇 Odéon

L'APPART (€€)
This two-storey house has a bar downstairs and a comfortable restaurant upstairs, reminiscent of a home library. Inventive dishes with a hint of the Mediterranean. The Sunday brunch also has the added bonus for parents—a kid's pastry workshop.
🔲 E3 ✉ 9–11 rue du Colisée 75008 (Champs Élysées) ☎ 01 53 75 42 00 🕐 Daily 🚇 Franklin D. Roosevelt

L'AVENUE (€€)
One of the hippest places in town, popular with film stars and models. Chocoholics will be tempted by the half-baked chocolate cake.
🔲 D4/E4 ✉ 41 avenue Montaigne 75008 (Champs Élysées) ☎ 01 40 70 14 91 🕐 Daily until 1am 🚇 Alma-Marceau

LES GRANDES MARCHES (€€)
Near the Opéra Bastille, with modern interior and innovative French cuisine, including caramel-coated monkfish. Known for its seafood platters.
🔲 Off map at Q8 ✉ 6 place de la Bastille 75012 ☎ 01 43 42 90 32 🕐 Daily 🚇 Bastille

MAN RAY (€€)
Hollywood actors, Sean Penn, Johnny Depp and John Malkovich launched this restaurant, with its Asian-inspired furnishings and mini-waterfall. The cuisine has French, Japanese and Thai flavours.
🔲 D4 ✉ 34 rue Marbeuf 75008 (Champs Élysées) ☎ 01 56 88 36 36 🕐 Daily 🚇 Franklin D. Roosevelt

MARKET (€€)
A large choice of oysters and fusion food by chef Jean-Georges Vongerichten. Highlights include black truffle pizza and the 'black plate' hors d'oeuvre selection.
🔲 F3 ✉ 15 avenue Matignon (Champs Élysées) ☎ 01 56 43 40 90 🕐 Daily 🚇 Franklin D. Roosevelt

VINS DES PYRÉNÉES (€€)
This wine shop turned bistro offers its young trendy clientele good food in a lively, convivial atmosphere.
🔲 Q8 ✉ 25 rue Beautreillis 75004 (Marais/Bastille) ☎ 01 42 72 64 94 🕐 Closed Sat lunch 🚇 Bastille, Sully Morland

ZE KITCHEN GALLERIE (€€)
Three good reasons to try this chic restaurant: the elegant contemporary décor, the fashionable clientele and the inventive cuisine by one of Guy Savoy's former assistants.
🔲 L8 ✉ 24 rue des Grands Augustins 75006 (Quartier Latin) ☎ 01 44 32 00 32 🕐 Closed Sat lunch, Sun 🚇 St-Michel

LA COUPOLE
Horror struck Parisian hearts in the mid-1980s when it was announced that La Coupole (▶ 66) had been bought by property developers and several floors were to be added on top. This happened, but the famous old murals (by Juan Gris, Soutine, Chagall, Delaunay and many more) have been reinstated, the red-velvet seats preserved and the art-deco lights duly restored. The 1920s interior is now a historic monument.

Asian Restaurants

THE 13TH ARRONDISSEMENT

The Paris Chinese community is spread through Belleville, where it coexists with Arabs and Africans; through the 3rd *arrondissement*, where invisible sweatshops churn out cheap leather goods; and above all through the 13th *arrondissement* (🚇 Tolbiac, Porte d'Ivry). At the latter, Chinese New Year is celebrated with dragon parades in late January or early February. The area offers a fantastic array of Indochinese and Chinese restaurants and soup kitchens—all at budget prices.

BANYAN (€€)

Oth Sombath (former chef of the Blue Elephant) now runs this small, convivial restaurant serving delicious Thai cuisine such as steamed sea bass with lime, seafood marinated with citronella and chocolate nems.

✚ Off map at B11 ✉ 24 place Etienne Pernet 75015 (Vaugirard) ☎ 01 40 60 09 31 🕐 Closed Sun 🚇 Félix Faure

BENKAY (€€)

A modern Japanese restaurant with panoramic views from the 4th floor of the Novotel Paris Tour Eiffel. Good *teppanyaki*. The set lunch menus are reasonably priced.

✚ Off map ✉ 61 quai de Grenelle 75015 (Vaugirard/ Grenelle) ☎ 01 40 58 21 26 🕐 Daily 🚇 Bir Hakeim

CHIENG-MAI (€€)

Elegant Thai restaurant, and one of the best in town, with charming service and subtle food. Always popular, so reserve in advance.

✚ M9 ✉ 12 rue Frédéric-Sauton 75005 (Latin Quarter/ Saint-Michel) ☎ 01 43 25 45 45 🕐 Daily, closed part of Aug 🚇 Maubert-Mutualité

GOA (€)

Good Indian food a stone's throw from the Champ de Mars: a selection of curries, lamb with coconut, all at resonable prices.

✚ D7 ✉ 19 rue Augereau 75007 (Invalides) ☎ 01 45 55 26 20 🕐 Closed Sun 🚇 École Militaire

KHUN AKORN (€€)

Highly flavoured Thai cuisine combined with tasteful surroundings and a pleasant terrace for spring and summer.

✚ Off map at Q9 ✉ 8 avenue de Taillebourg 75011 (Nation) ☎ 01 43 56 20 03 🕐 Closed Mon 🚇 Nation

NEW NIOULLAVILLE (€)

Vast Hong Kong-style restaurant with a long menu specializing in Chinese, Laotian, Thai and Vietnamese cuisine .

✚ Off map at Q4 ✉ 32–34 rue de l'Orillon 75011 (Belleville) ☎ 01 40 21 96 18 🕐 Daily 🚇 Belleville

TAN DINH (€€)

Good quality Vietnamese cuisine, in an elegantly designed restaurant situated just behind the Musée d'Orsay. Impressive wine list and polished service.

✚ H7 ✉ 60 rue de Verneuil 75007 (Saint-Germain-des-Prés) ☎ 01 45 44 04 84 🕐 Closed Sun, Aug 🚇 Rue du Bac

YUGARAJ (€€)

One of Paris's best Indian restaurants. Discreet and elegant, with friendly Sri Lankan waiters. Taditional curries plus more surprising combinations.

✚ L7 ✉ 14 rue Dauphine 75006 (Île de la Cité/Pont Neuf) ☎ 01 43 26 44 91 🕐 Closed Mon, Thu lunch 🚇 Pont Neuf

ZEN (€€)

For some of the best sushi in Paris in plush decor. Wash it down with the house white, but be warned—the wine list is rather pricey.

✚ L6 ✉ 18 rue du Louvre 75001 (Les Halles) ☎ 01 42 86 95 05 🕐 Closed Sun lunch, Mon, part of Aug 🚇 Louvre-Rivoli

Arab Restaurants

404 (€€)
In the same ownership as Momo off London's Regent Street, this very fashionable Moroccan restaurant with its chic Berber decor offers excellent North African cuisine.

🔢 P5 ✉ 69 rue des Gravilliers 75003 (Marais/République) ☎ 01 42 74 57 81 🕐 Daily. Closed Aug 🚇 Arts et Métiers

AL DAR (€€)
Luxurious Lebanese restaurant, with a terrific selection of *mezze* and excellent couscous. Take-away section.

🔢 M9 ✉ 8–10 rue Frédéric-Sauton 75005 (Latin Quarter/Saint-Michel) ☎ 01 43 25 17 15 🕐 Daily 🚇 Maubert-Mutualité

L'ATLAS (€€)
Fabulous kitsch juxtaposition of Louis XIII chairs and Moroccan mosaics. Modern interpretations of sophisticated North African cooking served with genuine smiles.

🔢 N9 ✉ 12 boulevard Saint-Germain 75005 (Latin Quarter/Saint-Michel) ☎ 01 44 07 23 66 🕐 Closed Tue lunch, Mon 🚇 Maubert-Mutualité

CHEZ OMAR (€)
Generous couscous and grilled meats in a friendly, spacious and buzzing setting. Popular; reserve for dinner or arrive early.

🔢 Q5 ✉ 47 rue de Bretagne 75003 (Marais/Republique) ☎ 01 42 72 36 26 🕐 Closed Sun lunch 🚇 Arts et Métiers

LE MANSOURIA (€€)
Authentic Moroccan restaurant offering some of the city's best couscous and *pastilla*. Often busy.

🔢 Off map at Q8 ✉ 11 rue Faidherbe 75011 (Bastille/Nation) ☎ 01 43 71 00 16 🕐 Closed Mon, Tue lunch, Sun 🚇 Faidherbe Chaligny

NOURA (€€)
Stylish, busy Lebanese snack bar with take-away service; brother of the plush Noura Pavillon (☎ 01 47 20 33 33) down the road.

🔢 C4 ✉ 27 avenue Marceau 75116 (Champs Élysées) ☎ 01 47 23 02 20 🕐 Daily 🚇 Alma-Marceau

TANJIA (€€)
Excellent Moroccan cuisine in a beautiful dining room with a fountain. The lounge club in the basement has divan beds and hookah pipes.

🔢 E3 ✉ 23 rue de Ponthieu 75008 (Champs Élysées) ☎ 01 42 25 95 00 🕐 Closed Sat, Sun lunch 🚇 Franklin D. Roosevelt

TIMGAD (€€€)
One of the best-known Arab restaurants in France. Spectacular Moorish decor. Delicate *pastilla*, perfect couscous, attentive service. Reserve ahead.

🔢 A1 ✉ 21 rue Brunel 75017 (Etoile/Ternes) ☎ 01 45 74 23 70 🕐 Daily 🚇 Argentine

WALLY LE SAHARIEN (€€)
Wally Chouaki offers a wonderful choice of *harira*, *pastilla*, stuffed sardines and, of course, couscous (Saharan). Delicious delicate pastries to finish.

🔢 L1 ✉ 36 rue Rodier 75009 (Pigalle) ☎ 01 42 85 51 90 🕐 Closed Mon, Sun 🚇 Anvers

COUSCOUS AND *TAJINE*

Couscous is a mound of steamed semolina that is accompanied by a tureen of freshly cooked vegetables (onion, tomato, carrot, courgette (zucchini) and the meat (or not) of your choice, from grilled lamb kebabs (*brochettes*) to chicken or *merguez* (spicy sausages). *Tajine* is a delicious stew, traditionally cooked in a covered terracotta dish, that may combine lamb and prunes, or chicken, pickled lemon and olives.

Italian Restaurants

CULINARY CONNECTIONS

It is said that Cathérine de Médicis, the Italian wife of Henri II, invented French cuisine in the 16th century—though Gallic opinions may differ. Italian cuisine in today's Paris is, not surprisingly, very much a pizza–pasta affair, and authentic dishes are rare. However, with a bit of dedication you can find some excellent exponents of Italian cuisine.

BEL CANTO (€€)

Relax and enjoy a selection of arias from Italian opera and Neapolitan songs with piano accompaniment while feasting on fine Italian cuisine.

➕ N8 ✉ 72 quai de l'Hôtel de Ville 75004 (facing Île St-Louis) ☎ 01 42 78 30 18 🕐 Daily, dinner only Ⓜ Pont Marie

CASA BINI (€€)

Chic but relaxed Tuscan-style trattoria specializes in north Italian dishes.

➕ K8 ✉ 36 rue Grégoire-de-Tours 75006 (Saint-Michel) ☎ 01 46 34 05 60 🕐 Daily Ⓜ Odéon

CAFÉ BACI (€€)

Located north of the place des Vosges, this restaurant serving mouth-watering Italian dishes is a popular haunt of film and theatre actors and directors.

➕ Q7 ✉ 36 rue de Turenne 75003 (Marais) ☎ 01 42 71 36 70 🕐 Daily Ⓜ Chemin Vert

CARUSO (€€)

Authentic cuisine from the south of Italy and wines to match, all served in appropriate surroundings: stone décor, warm welcome from the owner.

➕ Q8 ✉ 3 rue de Turenne 75003 (Marais) ☎ 01 42 77 06 98 🕐 Daily Ⓜ St-Paul

FINDI (€€)

Modern decor meets traditional Italian cusine, including Parma ham, homemade pasta and a wide range of *carpaccio* with the effect of attracting an elegant clientele.

➕ C4 ✉ 24 avenue George V 75008 (Champs Élysées) ☎ 01 47 20 14 78 🕐 Daily Ⓜ Alma-Marceau

GLI ANGELI (€€)

Reasonably priced Italian fare near the Place des Vosges featuring regional classics and all-Italian wine list. Be sure to reserve ahead.

➕ Q7 ✉ 5 rue Saint-Gilles 75003 (Marais) ☎ 01 42 71 05 80 🕐 Daily noon–2.30, 7.30–11.30 Ⓜ Chemin-Vert

SASSO (€€)

Delicious Italian cusine at reasonable prices. Alternatively, try the owners' newest restaurant Lei at 17 avenue de la Motte-Picquet 7th.

➕ Off map at G11 ✉ 36 rue Raymond Losserand 75014 (Montparnasse) ☎ 01 42 18 00 38 🕐 Closed Sun, Mon Ⓜ Pernety

SORMANI (€€€)

Just north of the Arc de Triomphe, this elegant restaurant, renowned for inspirational modern cooking, is popular with wealthy Parisians.

➕ B2 ✉ 4 rue du Général-de-Lanrezac 75017 (Champs Élysées) ☎ 01 43 80 13 91 🕐 Closed Sat, Sun, Aug Ⓜ Charles de Gaulle-Étoile

STRESA (€€)

Fashionable isn't the word. Couturiers drop in here for a quick pasta or risotto. The restaurant is run with gusto by Neapolitan twins. Reserve ahead.

➕ D4 ✉ 7 rue Chambiges 75008 (Champs Élysées) ☎ 01 47 23 51 62 🕐 Closed Sat dinner, Sun Ⓜ Alma-Marceau

Other Tasty Options

LE BAR À SOUPES (€)

Six fresh soups are offered
each day, including a
coconut milk and carrot,
and pumpkin and bacon.

✚ Off map at Q8 ✉ 33 rue de
Charonne 75011 (Bastille)
☎ 01 43 57 53 79 ⏰ Closed
Sun 🚇 Ledru Rollin, Bastille

MA BOURGOGNE (€€)

Hearty, unpretentious
food perfect for a summer
lunch or dinner. Or just
stop for a drink.

✚ Q7 ✉ 19 place des Vosges
75004 (Marais/Bastille) ☎ 01
42 78 44 64 ⏰ Daily
🚇 Chemin Vert

CAFÉ DE L'INDUSTRIE (€–€€)

Spacious, relaxed café-
restaurant/tea room that
serves up simple,
reasonable food.

✚ Off map at Q8 ✉ 16 rue
Saint-Sabin 75011 (Bastille)
☎ 01 47 00 13 53 ⏰ Daily
until 1.30am 🚇 Bastille

CHEZ IMOGÈNE (€)

Give your taste buds a
treat in this authentic
Breton crêperie serving a
wide selection of savoury
and sweet crêpes all
washed down with tangy
Breton cider.

✚ Off map at Q5 ✉ 25 rue
Jean-Pierre Timbaud 75011
(République) ☎ 01 48 07 14
59 ⏰ Closed Mon lunch, Sun
🚇 Oberkampf

LE FOUQUET'S (€€€)

A Parisian institution on
the Champs Élysées and a
place to see and be seen.
A snack menu operates in
the bar or on the terrace.

✚ C3/D3 ✉ 99 avenue des
Champs-Élysées 75008 (Champs
Élysées) ☎ 01 47 23 50 50
⏰ Daily 🚇 George V

LA GALERIE (€–€€)

Pleasant relief from the
Montmartre tourist
haunts. Set lunch and
dinner menus are very
good value. Friendly.

✚ Montmartre map ✉ 16 rue
Tholozé 75018 (Pigalle) ☎ 01
42 59 25 76 ⏰ Closed Tue
dinner 🚇 Abbesses

GAYA RIVE GAUCHE (€€)

Fashionable and popular
where the best and
freshest fish is prepared in
an uncomplicated manner.

✚ H7 ✉ 44 rue du Bac 75007
(Saint-Germain-des-Prés) ☎ 01
45 44 73 73 ⏰ Closed Sun,
Mon, 2 weeks Aug 🚇 Rue du Bac

PICCOLO TEATRO (€)

This restaurant, a pioneer
of vegetarian cuisine,
offers flavours from all
over the world.

✚ P7 ✉ 6 rue des Ecouffes
75004 (Le Marais) ☎ 01 42 72
17 79 ⏰ Daily 🚇 St-Paul

LA ROTISSERIE D'EN FACE (€€)

Across the road from
Jacques Cagna's main
restaurant, the setting
here is lively, modern
and informal. Spit-roast
chicken, suckling pig
and grilled salmon.

✚ L8 ✉ 2 rue Christine
75006 (Saint-Michel) ☎ 01 43
26 40 98 ⏰ Closed Sat lunch,
Sun 🚇 Odéon, St-Michel

WILLI'S WINE BAR (€€)

Cheerful, British-owned
restaurant/wine bar with
an extensive wine list
and fresh cuisine.

✚ K4 ✉ 13 rue des Petits
Champs 75001 (Palais Royal-
Opéra) ☎ 01 42 61 05 09
⏰ Closed Sun 🚇 Palais-Royal,
Musée du Louvre

PHARAMOND

This restaurant, founded in
1832, is a sanctuary for lovers
of tripe, pigs' trotters and
andouillette. It was entirely
redecorated for the 1900
Exposition Universelle, and
most of this structure and
decoration has been
preserved. The pretty floral
and vegetal friezes that cover
the walls of the rooms once
adorned the entire four-storey
façade. Prices are high and
reservations are essential.

✚ M5 ✉ 24 rue de la
Grande Truanderie 75001
☎ 01 40 28 45 18 ⏰ Closed
Sun 🚇 Les Halles

Department Stores

OPENING HOURS

Parisian opening hours follow a Monday to Saturday pattern. Smaller shops generally open by 10am, sometimes closing for lunch, and shut at 7pm. The following pages show opening times when they vary from this norm. Avoid shopping on Saturdays when every citizen seems to hit the streets, and take advantage of department store late-opening nights. Chain stores such as Monoprix are useful when you need inexpensive household goods and even fashion accessories.

BERCY VILLAGE

This latest addition to Paris's shopping scene is located in the newly renovated Bercy district, across the Seine from the Bibliothèque Nationale François-Mitterrand. Some 20 boutiques, several restaurants and leisure activities in a village atmosphere.

➕ Off map at Q11 ✉ 28 rue François Truffaut 75012 ☎ 01 40 02 90 80 🕐 Daily 11–9 🚇 Cour Saint-Émilion

BHV (BAZAR DE L'HÔTEL DE VILLE)

Everything you can think of under one roof. This store opened in 1856.

➕ N7 ✉ 52–64 rue de Rivoli 75004 ☎ 01 42 74 90 00 🕐 Mon–Sat 9.30–7.30 (also Wed, Fri until 9) 🚇 Hôtel de Ville

LE BON MARCHÉ RIVE GAUCHE

Very *BCBG* (*bon chic bon genre*). Designer clothes, household linens and haberdashery. with specialist foods in a neighbouring building.

➕ H9 ✉ 22 rue de Sèvres 75007 ☎ 01 44 39 80 00 🕐 Mon, Tue, Wed, Fri 9.30–7, Thu 10–9, Sat 9.30–8 🚇 Sèvres-Babylone

FORUM DES HALLES

Underground complex on four levels where some 50 small ready-to-wear designers have their boutiques.

➕ M6 ✉ 1–7 rue Pierre-Lescot 75001 🚇 Châtelet, Les Halles

GALERIES LAFAYETTE

Under a giant glass dome, an enticing display of everything a home and its inhabitants need. Marginally better quality and pricier than Printemps. Top fashion designers are all represented and accessories are endless. Some departments are enormous, such as lingerie. There is a smaller branch near the Tour Montparnasse.

➕ J2 ✉ 40 boulevard Haussmann 75009 ☎ 01 42 82 34 56 🕐 Mon–Wed, Fri, Sat 9.30–7.30, Thu 9.30–9 🚇 Chaussée d'Antin

PRINTEMPS

A classic for men's and women's fashions, accessories, household goods, furniture, designer gadgets and more. The store is split into three sections—fashion (de la Mode), home (de la Maison) and menswear (de l'homme). Don't miss the lavish stained-glass cupola in Café Flo, on the 6th floor of Printemps de la Mode.

➕ H2–J2 ✉ 64 boulevard Haussmann 75009 ☎ 01 42 82 50 00 🕐 Mon–Wed, Fri, Sat 9.35–7 (also Thu until 10) 🚇 Havre-Caumartin

SAMARITAINE

Labyrinthine store largely occupying a superb 1904 construction with wonderful art-nouveau details. You can enjoy great panoramic views across the Seine from the rooftop (▶ 59) and there's also a café and restaurant.

➕ L6 ✉ 19 rue de la Monnaie 75001 ☎ 01 40 41 20 20 🕐 Mon–Sat 9.30–7 (also Thu until 9, Sat until 8) 🚇 Pont Neuf

Food & Wine

CHARCUTERIE LYONNAISE
The specialities of Lyon, including sublime *jambon persille* and sausages.
L1 58 rue des Martyrs 75009 01 48 78 96 45 Anvers

DUBOIS ET FILS
An overwhelming selection of cheeses (over 70 varieties of goat's cheese). Cheese tastings and delivery service. Try the top-quality Saint-Marcellin.
Off map at E1 80 rue de Tocqueville 75017 01 42 27 11 38 Malesherbes, Villiers

FAUCHON
The gourmet's paradise—at a price. Luxury delicatessen founded in 1886, offering only the best in spices, exotic fruit, tea, coffee, charcuterie, pâtisseries… and more.
H3 26 place de la Madeleine 75008 01 47 42 91 10 Madeleine

LA MAISON DU MIEL
Countless types of honey—chestnut, lavender, pine-tree, acacia—presented in a pretty, tiled interior dating from 1908. Also beeswax soap and candles.
H3 24 rue Vignon 75009 01 47 42 26 70 Madeleine

A LA MÈRE DE FAMILLE
Original 18th-century grocery shop with shelves laden with imaginatively created chocolates, jams and unusual groceries.
L2 35 rue du Faubourg, Montmartre 75009 01 47 70 83 69 Le Peletier, Cadet

LABEYRIE
Specializes in products from the Landes. Goose and duck livers, *foie gras*, truffles and dried mushrooms of all types.
Off map at A10 11 rue d'Auteuil 75016 01 42 24 17 62 Michel Ange-Auteuil, Église d'Auteuil

LENÔTRE
Famous for its fine foods and pastries. Don't misss the 'maccarre', a brightly coloured square macaroon.
Off map at F1 15 boulevard de Coucelles 75008 01 45 63 87 63 Daily Villiers

MARIAGE FRÉRES
This teahouse, founded in 1854, is a Paris institution. Choose from hundreds of teas from all over the world, including some exclusive house blends.
P7 30 rue du Bourg-Tibourg 75004 01 42 72 28 11 Daily 10.30–7.30 Hôtel de Ville

NICOLAS
This wine shop, in Bercy, is part of a chain that offers a good selection of vintages. Bottles from their small vineyard collection are particularly good value. Have a taste!
Off map at Q9 24 Cour St-Emilion 01 44 74 62 65 Mon–Thu 9–8.30, Fri–Sun 10–9 Cour St-Emilion

OLIVIERS & CO
Dedicated to olive oil and related products—olive-oil flavoured biscuits, tapenade and bowls made from olive wood.
P7 47 rue Vieille du Temple 01 42 74 38 40 Daily 11–8 Hôtel de Ville

CHOCAHOLICS
Chocolate came to Europe via Spain from South America. Under Louis XIV it became a fashionable drink and was served three times a week at Versailles. Paris's first chocolate shop opened in 1659. Voltaire drank up to 12 cups a day, and Napoleon apparently had a penchant for chocolate first thing in the morning. But with their consumption of a mere 5.5kg (12lb) per person per annum, the French lag behind the Swiss, who consume an annual 10kg (22lb), and the Belgians at 7kg (15lb). Debauve & Gallais (J7 30 rue des Saints-Pères 75007 01 45 48 54 67 Saint-Germain-des-Prés) is an original wood-panelled 18th-century pharmacy that became a chocolate shop when the medicinal properties of cocoa were discovered.

Markets

FOOD MARKETS

Parisians shop daily for their fresh produce and perfectly ripe cheeses. Temporary food markets spring up on boulevards throughout the city on different days of the week (the Bastille Sunday market is particularly enormous), but permanent food markets exist on rue Poncelet (🚉 C1), rue Daguerre (🚉 Off map) and on rue de Buci on the Left Bank (🚉 K8). All keep provincial lunch hours, so avoid 1–4pm.

MARCHÉ D'ALIGRE

Second-hand clothes, crockery and bric-a-brac in the middle of a large, low-priced food market. Has the feeling of a Moroccan bazaar.
🚉 Off map at Q8 ✉ place d'Aligre 75012 🕐 Tue–Sun 7.30am–12.30pm 🚉 Ledru Rollin

MARCHÉ DU BOULEVARD RASPAIL

A strictly organic market, with flavousome fruit and vegetables, honey, bread and wine.
🚉 H9 ✉ boulevard Raspail 75006 (Saint-Germain-des-Prés) 🕐 Sun 9–1 🚉 Rennes

MARCHÉ AUX FLEURS

A charming flower and plant market, with everything from delicate orchids to 2-m (6-ft) tall eucalyptus trees.
🚉 M8 ✉ place Louis Lépine 75004 🕐 Mon–Sat 8–7 (bird market on Sun) 🚉 Cité

MARCHÉ DE MONTREUIL

Jeans and jackets start at the Métro. Persevere across the bridge for domestic appliances, carpets, bric-a-brac and some great second-hand stuff. Morning is best.
🚉 Off map at Q8 ✉ avenue du Professeur André Lemière 75020 🕐 Sat–Mon 7–7:30 🚉 Porte de Montreuil

MARCHÉ AUX PUCES DE SAINT-OUEN

(▶ 44)

MARCHÉ DE LA RUE LEPIC

Up a steep hill, but worth the effort. Head down the other side of the hill to the rue du Poteau (🚉 Jules-Joffrin) for African foods.
🚉 Montmartre map ✉ rue Lepic 75018 🕐 Tue–Sat 9–1, 4–7, Sun 9–1 🚉 Abbesses

MARCHÉ DE LA RUE MONTORGUEIL

A microcosm of what was Les Halles food market (now moved to Rungis in the suburbs), this is a marble-paved pedestrian street with atmosphere and plenty of trendy little bars and lunch places.
🚉 M5 ✉ rue Montorgueil 75001 🕐 Tue–Sat 9–1, 4–7, Sun 9–1 🚉 Les Halles

MARCHÉ DE LA RUE MOUFFETARD

A tourist classic straggling down a winding, narrow, hilly street. Wonderful array of fruit and vegetables, and plenty of aromatic cheeses and *charcuterie*. Good café stops en route.
🚉 M11 ✉ rue Mouffetard 75005 🕐 Tue, Thu, Sat 9–1, 4–7 🚉 Monge

MARCHÉ AUX TIMBRES

Philatelists zoom in here to buy and sell their miniature treasures.
🚉 E4 ✉ rond-point des Champs-Elysées 75008 🕐 Thu, Sat, Sun and holidays 9–7 🚉 Franklin D. Roosevelt

MARCHÉ DE VANVES

Popular with yuppies hot on 1950s and art-deco styles. Second-hand furniture, bric-a-brac, paintings, prints and some ethnic items.
🚉 Off map at F11 ✉ avenue Georges Lafeuestre, avenue Marc Sangnier 75014 🕐 Sat–Sun 7–7.30 🚉 Porte de Vanves

Art & Antiques

CARRÉ RIVE GAUCHE

Home to some of Paris's top antiques dealers selling archaeological pieces, Louis XIV, XV, Empire, Japanese scrolls, 19th-century bronzes, astrolabes and prints.
🚇 H7–J7 ✉ rue du Bac, quai Voltaire, rue des Saints-Pères, rue de l'Université 75007 ☎ no phone; www.carrerivegauche.com 🕐 Tue–Sat 10.30–7 🚇 Rue du Bac

GALERIE CAPTIER

Chinese furniture, from the 17th to 19th centuries and old Japanese screens.
🚇 J7 ✉ 33 rue de Beaune 75007 ☎ 01 42 61 00 57 🕐 Tue–Sat 10.30–7, Mon 2.30–7 🚇 Rue du Bac

GALERIE DOCUMENTS

Original posters and etchings from 1890 to 1940 by such masters as Toulouse-Lautrec and Alphonse Mucha.
🚇 K8 ✉ 53 rue de Seine 75006 ☎ 01 43 54 50 68 🕐 Tue–Sat 10.30–7, Mon 2.30–7 🚇 Odéon, Mabillon

GALERIE DURAND-DESSERT

Spectacular conversion of an old Bastille mattress factory into a conceptual art mecca.
🚇 Off map at Q8 ✉ 28 rue de Lappe 75011 ☎ 01 48 06 92 23 🕐 Tue–Sat 11–7 🚇 Bastille

GALERIE DU JOUR AGNÈS B

Fashion meets art at this gallery, with young, hip talent on view in photography and painting.
🚇 N6 ✉ 44 rue Quincampoix 75004 ☎ 01 44 54 55 90 🕐 Tue–Sat noon–7 🚇 Rambuteau

LOUVRE DES ANTIQUAIRES

Huge, modernized complex of antiques shops. You'll find everything from Eastern carpets to Lalique glass, jewellery, furniture, silver, porcelain and paintings. Good quality but expect high prices.
🚇 L6 ✉ 2 place du Palais-Royal 75001 ☎ 01 42 97 27 27; www.louvre-antiquaires.com 🕐 Tue–Sun 11–7 (closed Sun in July and Aug) 🚇 Palais-Royal; Musée du Louvre

SALLE RASPAIL

A curious mixture of items from the 18th, 19th and 20th centuries.
🚇 Off map at J11 ✉ 224 boulevard Raspail 75014 ☎ 01 56 54 11 90 🕐 Tue–Fri 11–8, Sat 11–7 🚇 Raspail

VILLAGE SAINT-PAUL

A cluster of antiques and bric-a-brac shops opening onto an enclosed square. Shops continue down the streets on either side, with everything from Asian textiles to glass, old furniture or clothes.
🚇 Q8 ✉ rue Saint-Paul, rue Charlemagne 75004 🕐 Thu–Mon 11–7 🚇 St-Paul

XXO

XXO (Extra Extra Original) sells 1950s to 1980s furniture, including Colombo chairs, lip-shaped sofas etc... It also hires out to the movie industry.
🚇 Off map at Q1 ✉ 78 rue de la Fraternité 93230, Romainville ☎ 01 48 18 08 88; www.xxo.com 🚇 No Métro or RER. Take the A3 from Porte de Bagnolet to Romainville

GALLERIES

Even if you cannot afford to invest in contemporary art, Paris offers a good window on the latest movements. Art has traditionally centred on the Left Bank around the rue de Seine, but today the more avant-garde galleries spread east from the Centre Georges Pompidou area through the Marais to the Bastille. Pick up a free gallery map at one of the galleries and follow the creative route.

AUCTION HOUSE

Hôtel Druot (✉ 9 rue Druot ☎ 01 48 00 20 20) is the city's main auction house. Anything can come under the hammer– antique jewellery, silverware, toys, household items, rare maps, even wines.
Forthcoming sales are listed in the *Gazette de l'Hôtel Druot*, sold at newsagents. Antiques hunters should also stroll the Seine quaysides.

Books & Records

BRENTANO'S
Well-stocked American bookshop with good travel and art sections at the back. Bilingual staff.
➕ J4 ✉ 37 avenue de l'Opéra 75001 ☎ 01 42 61 52 50
Ⓜ Opéra, Pyramides

LA CHAMBRE CLAIRE
Excellent photography bookshop with a wide range of international publications. Occasional exhibitions.
➕ K9 ✉ 14 rue Saint-Sulpice 75006 ☎ 01 46 34 04 31
🕐 Tue–Sat Ⓜ Odéon

FNAC
One of the main branches of this firmly established cultural chain. Books, records, cameras, audio, computer accessories. Fair-price policy reigns.
➕ H10 ✉ 136 rue de Rennes 75006 ☎ 01 49 54 30 00
Ⓜ St-Placide

GALIGNANI
Pleasantly traditional, spacious bookshop brimming with laden tables and shelves. Large stock of English, German and French literature and art books.
➕ J5 ✉ 224 rue de Rivoli 75001 ☎ 01 42 60 76 07
Ⓜ Tuileries

LA HUNE
Excellent literary bookshop with extensive art and architecture section. Both French and imported books. Great for late-night browsing—open until midnight Monday to Saturday and to 8pm on Sunday.
➕ J8 ✉ 170 boulevard Saint-Germain 75006 ☎ 01 45 48 35 85 Ⓜ Saint-Germain-des-Prés

LIBRAIRIE GOURMANDE
Cookery and gastronomy titles new and old serve up treats for gourmets.
➕ M9 ✉ 4 rue Dante 75005 ☎ 01 43 54 37 27 Ⓜ St-Michel, Maubert Mutualité

SHAKESPEARE AND COMPANY
A charming English bookshop that stocks new and used books. There is also a small library upstairs.
➕ M9 ✉ 37 rue de la Bûcherie 75005 ☎ 01 43 26 96 50 🕐 Daily noon–midnight Ⓜ St-Michel

W. H. SMITH
Paris branch of one of the UK market leaders, offering a vast selection of English language titles, including books, magazines and videos.
➕ H4/H5 ✉ 248 rue de Rivoli 75001 ☎ 01 44 77 88 99 Ⓜ Concorde

VILLAGE VOICE
One of the best selections of new and hard to find fiction/non-fiction in English. Poetry readings and guest author appearances.
➕ K8 ✉ 6 rue Princesse 75006 ☎ 01 46 33 36 47 Ⓜ Mabillon

VIRGIN MEGASTORE
Enormous palace of records with generous opening hours, plus a chic café. Another branch is in the Carrousel du Louvre, 99 rue de Rivoli.
➕ D3 ✉ 52–60 Champs Élysées 75008 ☎ 01 49 53 50 00 🕐 Daily 10am–midnight, Sun noon–midnight Ⓜ Franklin D. Roosevelt

SUNDAY OPENINGS

Sundays now have a strong consumer element to them at the new marble-clad Carrousel du Louvre, perfect for a rainy day. Offerings include a Virgin record/bookshop, a newsagent with a wide international selection, Bodum kitchenware, Nature et Découvertes (a fashionably 'ecological' toy and gadget shop), a stylish optician and various boutiques. The entrance is from 99 rue de Rivoli or by the Carrousel arch in the Louvre.

Miscellaneous

L'ART DU BUREAU
High-tech and designer accessories for the desktop; tasteful stationery.

⊞ P7 ✉ 47 rue des Francs Bourgeois 75004 ☎ 01 48 87 57 97 Ⓜ St-Paul

LA DROGUERIE
This gem of a haberdasher's shop sells everything you'll need to make your own jewellery, knit or customize accessories for your home.

⊞ M5 ✉ 9 rue du Jour 75001 ☎ 01 45 08 93 27 Ⓜ Les Halles

CHRISTIAN TORTU
Anemones, amaryllis and apple-blossom—this is the place for the ultimate bouquet. Beautiful, understated wrapping.

⊞ L8 ✉ 6 Carrefour de l'Odéon 75006 ☎ 01 43 26 02 56 Ⓜ Odéon

DEHILLERIN
Food-lover's paradise, brimming with copper pans, knives, bains-marie, sieves and more. Mail-order service.

⊞ L5 ✉ 18 rue Coquillière 75001 ☎ 01 42 36 53 13 Ⓜ Les Halles, Louvre-Rivoli

DIPTYQUE
Perfumed candles and *eau de toilette*, plus men's ties, scarves and superb glasses.

⊞ N9 ✉ 34 boulevard Saint-Germain 75005 ☎ 01 43 26 45 27 Ⓜ Maubert-Mutualité

IKUO
A tiny shop packed with interesting jewellery, mainly by Japanese creators. Good value.

⊞ L8 ✉ 11 rue des Grands-Augustins 75006 ☎ 01 43 29 56 39 Ⓜ St-Michel

NAÏLA DE MONBRISON
Gallery showing some of the most sought-after contemporary jewellery; designers include Marcial Berro, Gilles Jonemann, Giorgio Vigna.

⊞ G6 ✉ 6 rue de Bourgogne 75007 ☎ 01 47 05 11 15 Ⓜ Invalides, Assemblée Nationale

PAPIER +
Emporium of quality paper in endless subtle hues. Superbly bound books, files and bouquets of coloured pencils.

⊞ P8 ✉ 9 rue du Pont Louis-Philippe 75004 ☎ 01 42 77 70 49 Ⓜ Pont Marie

PARFUMS ET SILLAGES
An aromatic universe of perfumes, potpourris and essences based on floral, fruity and spicy themes.

⊞ H7 ✉ 84 bis rue de Grenelle 75007 ☎ 01 45 44 61 57 Ⓜ Rue du Bac

SEPHORA
A classy and slightly futuristic perfumery where the fragrances are displayed by alphabetical order.

⊞ D3 ✉ 70 avenue des Champs Élysées 75008 ☎ 01 53 93 22 50 Ⓜ Franklin D. Roosevelt

SI TU VEUX
Charming toy shop with affordable and interesting toys, games and dressing-up gear. Separate section devoted to teddy-bear-related items.

⊞ L4 ✉ 68 Galerie Vivienne 75002 ☎ 01 42 60 59 97 Ⓜ Bourse

WINDOW-SHOPPING

Some Parisian streets do not fit any convenient label and so make for intriguing window-shopping. Try rue Jean-Jacques Rousseau and Passage Véro-Dodat, rue Saint-Roch, rue Monsieur-le-Prince and parallel rue de l'Odéon, rue Saint-Sulpice, rue des Francs-Bourgeois and rue du Pont-Louis-Philippe or rue de la Roquette. For luxury goods take a stroll along the rue du Faubourg-Saint-Honoré.

ETHNIC ATTRACTIONS

Discerning food lovers suffering from a surfeit of delectable but outrageously priced French groceries should head for Paris's ethnic areas. For Indian products the Passage Brady is unbeatable, while the nearby rue d'Enghien harbours several Turkish grocery shops. Belleville offers both Arab and Chinese specialities, while the Goutte d'Or (Barbès) focuses on Africa. For a real taste of the Far East, go to the Chinese supermarket Tang Frères at 48 avenue d'Ivry in the 13th *arrondissement*.

Fashion

TOP DESIGNERS

No trip to Paris would be complete without a stroll down the rue du Faubourg-Saint-Honoré and the even more elegant shopping of the avenue Montaigne. A roll-call of top designers leaves one gaping at the style, and the prices.

AGNÈS B

Agnès B's fashion is the epitome of young Parisian chic. Sharply cut clothes with original details are her signature.

➕ M5 ✉ 6 rue du Jour 75001 ☎ 01 45 08 56 56 Ⓜ Les Halles

ANTIK BATIK

The place to shop for ethnic-chic fashions, including embroidered blouses, batik-printed stoles and even lingerie.

➕ Q7 ✉ 18 rue de Turenne 75004 ☎ 01 44 78 02 00 Ⓜ Hôtel de Ville, Bastille

ANTHONY PETO

The male answer to Marie Mercié (► 79). Inventive and wearable men's quality headgear from top hats to berets, all aimed at the young and hip.

➕ M5 ✉ 56 rue Tiquetonne 75002 ☎ 01 40 26 60 68 Ⓜ Étienne Marcel

AZZEDINE ALAÏA

Silhouette-hugging dresses as worn by Tina Turner, Grace Jones and various supermodels.

➕ P7 ✉ 7 rue de Moussy 75004 ☎ 01 42 72 19 19 Ⓜ Hôtel de Ville

BARBARA BUI

One of Paris's most talented young designers. Tailored jackets, fitted tops, tight trousers and an impressive collection of high-heeled shoes for the urban woman.

➕ M5 ✉ 23 rue Étienne-Marcel 75001 ☎ 01 40 26 43 65 Ⓜ Étienne-Marcel

BILL TORNADE

Bill Tornade's menswear is sober, yet modern and classy. The limited edition range gives a rather exclusive touch.

➕ L5 ✉ 44 rue Étienne Marcel 75002 ☎ 01 42 33 66 47 Ⓜ Étienne-Marcel

CHANEL

Classy yet sexy, Chanel's fashion embodies Parisian elegance.

➕ H4 ✉ 29 rue Cambon 75001 ☎ 01 42 86 28 00 Ⓜ Madeleine

COLETTE

The place to go for leading design in fashion and home furnishings. The water bar downstairs serves more than 100 brands of bottled water.

➕ J5 ✉ 213 rue Saint-Honoré 75001 ☎ 01 55 35 33 90 Ⓜ Tuileries, Pyramides

DIDIER LUDOT

Rare vintage designer clothes (Chanel, Dior, Balmain) and classic Hermès handbags. Picturesque location.

➕ K5 ✉ 24 Galerie Montpensier 75001 ☎ 01 42 96 06 56 Ⓜ Palais-Royal, Musée du Louvre

FRANCK ET FILS

Founded at the end of the 19th century, but now reinvented as an elegant boutique with the top names in fashions.

➕ Off map at A7 ✉ 80 rue de Passy 75016 ☎ 01 44 14 38 00 Ⓜ La Muette

L'HABILLEUR

Leftover designer stock at huge discounts. Plenty of choice, with helpful sales staff.

➕ Q6 ✉ 44 rue de Poitou 75003 ☎ 01 48 87 77 12 Ⓜ Saint-Sébastien-Froissart

IRIÉ

Superbly cut and
accessibly priced
separates; trendy, but
stand the test of time. A
pioneer on this discreet
street.

✚ J7 ✉ 8 rue du Pré-aux-
Clercs 75007 ☎ 01 42 61 18
28 Ⓜ St-Germain-des-Prés

ISABEL MARANT

Casual-chic at its best.
Isabel Marant has updated
Parisian elegance by
giving it a bohemian-
bourgeois twist. Funky
wearable clothes.

✚ Off map at Q8 ✉ 16 rue de
Charonne 75011 ☎ 01 49 29
71 55 Ⓜ Bastille, Ledru-Rollin

JUDITH LACROIX

This young designer made
a name for herself with
the success of her kids'
range, whose fabric
reproduced the layout of a
homework notebook. She
now also designs
womenswear.

✚ L1 ✉ 15 rue Hippolyte-
Lebas 75009 ☎ 01 42 82 12
50 Ⓜ Notre-Dame de Lorette

KOOKAI

Flagship shop of this fun,
trendy chain, popular with
the young.

✚ Off map at A5 ✉ 2 rue
Gustave-Courbet 75016 ☎ 01 47
55 18 00 Ⓜ Rue de la Pompe

LE SHOP

Shop to the sound of
techno in this massive
industrial space, home to
the most fashionable
brands of streetwear,
including Carhartt, Loona
and Lady Soul. Also has a
bar on site.

✚ L4/L5 ✉ 3 rue d'Argout
75002 ☎ 01 40 28 95 94
Ⓜ Etienne Marcel, Seutier

MARIE MERCIÉ

Extravagant hats for
women, from classic to
theatrical. The men's store
is near Les Halles at 56
rue Tiquetonne (✚ M5).

✚ K9 ✉ 23 rue Saint-Sulpice
75006 ☎ 01 43 26 45 83
Ⓜ Odéon

MI-PRIX

Designer clothes at a
fraction of the price; also
shoes by Michel Perry.

✚ Off map at A11 ✉ 27
boulevard Victor 75015 ☎ 01
48 28 42 48 Ⓜ Porte de
Versailles

SCOOTER

To get that real Les Halles
look, drop in here for the
latest accessories: ethnic,
1960s/70s revival
transformed into jewellery,
bags and clothes.

✚ M5 ✉ 10 rue de Turbigo
75001 ☎ 01 45 08 50 54
Ⓜ Etienne-Marcel

SONIA RYKIEL

Ready-to-wear fashion
house with economy range
of accessories and
cosmetics.

✚ J8 ✉ 175 boulevard Saint-
Germain 75006 ☎ 01 49 54
60 60 Ⓜ Saint-Germain-des-Prés

SOULEIADO

Cheerful range of fabrics,
table linen and cushions
in bright Provençal prints.

✚ K8/K9 ✉ 3 rue du
Lobineau 75006 ☎ 01 43 54
62 25 Ⓜ Mabillon

VICTOIRE

Cool salon for hot
fashions. Features the
best collections of the
current designer labels.

✚ L4/L5 ✉ 2 rue du Mail
75002 ☎ 01 42 96 46 76
Ⓜ Bourse, Palais-Royal

FASHION HUBS

The fact that women's high
fashion is concentrated in just
three complexes makes
clothes shopping, or mere
window-gazing, easy. The hub
of place des Victoires (home
to Kenzo, Stephane Kélian,
Plein Sud and Victoire)
continues along the rue
Étienne-Marcel and towards
Les Halles. The Marais's
enticing offerings run between
the rue de Sévigné, rue des
Rosiers, place des Vosges and
side streets. Saint-Germain
burgeons along and off the
boulevard, rue de Grenelle
and continues up the
boulevard Raspail.

ZEN CUTS

Issey Miyake reigns OK! His
sculptural, finely pleated
creations in imaginative
synthetics are sold at 3 Place
des Vosges 75004 (☎ 01 48
87 01 86).

Concerts, Jazz Clubs & Nightclubs

INEXPENSIVE CONCERTS

Numerous classical music concerts are held in churches—try Saint-Eustache, Saint-Germain-des-Prés, Saint-Julien-le-Pauvre, Saint-Louis-en-l'Île, Saint-Roch and Saint-Séverin. Seats are reasonably priced and the quality of music is sometimes very high. In May to September free concerts are held in parks all over the city. Programmes are available at the Office du Tourisme or the Hôtel de Ville.

RECITALS

Chopin gave his last recital at what is now the most prestigious venue on the classical circuit and home to the Orchestre de Paris—the Salle Pleyel (✉ 252 rue du Faubourg-Saint-Honoré 75008 ☎ 01 45 61 53 00). It is the venue for many of Paris's major concerts, often with world-famous soloists, and for recordings. The Salle Gaveau (✉ 45 rue de la Boétie 75008 ☎ 01 49 53 05 07; www.sallegaveau.com), which opened in 1907, also attracts top international opera singers and pianists.

CONCERT VENUES

AUDITORIUM DU LOUVRE

A high-quality and varied programme of lunchtime and evening concerts in an impressive 420-seat auditorium beneath the Louvre's pyramid.
➕ K6 ✉ Le Louvre (entrance by the pyramid) 75001 ☎ 01 40 20 55 55; www.louvre.fr
Ⓜ Louvre-Rivoli

CAFÉ DE LA DANSE

Pop, rock and world music in an auditorium that feels cosy, despite having room for 500 people. Also some theatre and dance.
➕ Off map at Q8 ✉ 5 passage Louis-Philippe 75011 ☎ 01 47 00 57 59; www.cafedeladanse.com
Ⓜ Bastille

CITÉ DE LA MUSIQUE

Accessible classical, jazz and world music at this concert hall in an out-of-the-way location.
➕ Off map at Q1 ✉ 221 avenue Jean-Jaurès 75019 ☎ 01 44 84 44 84; www.cite-musique.fr Ⓜ Porte de Pantin

OPÉRA BASTILLE

Paris's 'people's' opera house with its five moveable stages is a technological feat in itself. Opera, recitals, dance and even theatre.
➕ Off map at Q8 ✉ 120 rue de Lyon 75012 ☎ 08 92 89 90 90; www.opera-de-paris.fr
Ⓜ Bastille

OPÉRA COMIQUE

Sumptuously decorated opera house that stages light opera, dance and sometimes theatre.

➕ K3 ✉ place Boieldieu 75002 ☎ 08 25 00 00 58; www.opera-comique.com
Ⓜ Richelieu-Drouot

THÉÂTRE DES CHAMPS-ÉLYSÉES

Top international orchestras play in a stately setting. High-quality programme. Expensive.
➕ D5 ✉ 15 avenue Montaigne 75008 ☎ 01 49 52 50 50; www.theatrechamps elysees.fr Ⓜ Alma-Marceau

THÉÂTRE DU CHÂTELET

Varied schedule of opera, symphonic music and dance. Inexpensive seats for lunchtime concerts.
➕ M7 ✉ place du Châtelet 75001 ☎ 01 40 28 28 40; www.chatelet-theatre.com
Ⓜ Châtelet

THÉÂTRE DE LA VILLE

Modern theatre with an adventurous programme of contemporary dance, avant-garde music, theatre and early evening recitals of world music.
➕ M7 ✉ place du Châtelet 75004 ☎ 01 42 74 22 77;
Ⓜ Châtelet

JAZZ CLUBS

BILBOQUET

Classic jazz venue and restaurant in Saint-Germain-des-Prés; concerts at 9.30pm.
➕ J8 ✉ 13 rue Saint-Benoît 75006 ☎ 01 45 48 81 84
Ⓒ Closed Mon Ⓜ Saint-Germain-des-Prés

CAVEAU DE LA HUCHETTE

Still going strong, a smoky basement bar with dancing and live jazz from 9.30pm.

✚ M8 ✉ 5 rue de la Huchette
75005 ☎ 01 43 26 65 05
Ⓜ St-Michel

DUC DES LOMBARDS

Prestigious jazz musicians
regularly play in this cosy
club in Les Halles.
✚ M6 ✉ 42 rue des Lombards
75001 ☎ 01 42 33 22 88
Ⓒ Closed Sun Ⓜ Châtelet

NEW MORNING

One of Paris's top
jazz/blues/soul bars with a
good atmosphere. Reserve
for top names.
✚ N3 ✉ 7/9 rue des Petites-
Écuries 75010 ☎ 01 45 23
51 41 Ⓒ Nightly Ⓜ Château
d'Eau

PETIT JOURNAL
MONTPARNASSE

This club, sister venue to
the Petit Journal on
boulevard St-Michel, has
hosted some of France's
best-loved jazz musicians,
and you can enjoy high-
quality food, too.
✚ Off map at G11 ✉ 13 rue
Commandant-Mouchotte 75014
☎ 01 43 21 56 70 Ⓒ Closed
Sun Ⓜ Montparnasse-Bienvenüe

LE SUNSET

Part of the Les Halles
cluster, a restaurant-bar
with good jazz from 10pm
until the small hours.
Reasonably priced food.
✚ M6 ✉ 60 rue des Lombards
75001 ☎ 01 40 26 46 60
Ⓒ Closed Sun Ⓜ Châtelet

NIGHTCLUBS

L'AMNESIA

A choice of styles on
different nights from
House music of the 1990s
to R'n'B and current
House.
✚ Off map at G11 ✉ 24 rue

de l'Arrivée 7501 ☎ 01 56 80
37 37 Ⓒ Closed Mon
Ⓜ Montparnasse-Bienvenüe

LES BAINS

This club was once
number one for the
celebrity set and is still a
good place to groove.
✚ N5 ✉ 7 rue du Bourg-
l'Abbé 75003 ☎ 01 48 87
01 80 Ⓒ Closed Sun, Mon
Ⓜ Étienne-Marcel

DUPLEX

A club for well-to-do
twenty-somethings, (smart
dress required). Bowling
alley.
✚ B2 ✉ 2 bis, avenue Foch
75016 ☎ 01 45 00 45 00
Ⓒ Closed Mon Ⓜ Charles de
Gaulle-Étoile

LATINA CAFÉ

The complete Latino
experience, with live
bands, DJs and even salsa
classes (on Sundays). The
three-floor venue has a
bar, restaurant and club.
✚ C3 ✉ 114 avenue des
Champs Élysées 75008 ☎ 01
42 89 98 89 Ⓒ Nightly
Ⓜ George V

QUEEN

A gay club that also
attracts a straight and
trendy crowd. House and
garage music, mixed by
international DJs.
✚ C3/D3 ✉ 102 avenue des
Champs Élysées 75008 ☎ 01
53 89 08 90 Ⓒ Nightly
Ⓜ George V

WAGG

House and dance music in
a cosy venue. Popular with
mid 20s to mid 30s.
✚ K8 ✉ 62 rue Mazarine
75006 ☎ 01 55 42 22 00
Ⓒ Closed Sun–Tue Ⓜ Odéon,
St-Germain-des-Prés

CLUBS AND RAVES

Paris clubbing is both serious
and fickle—serious because no
truly cool Parisian turns up
before midnight, and fickle
because mass loyalties change
rapidly. Most clubs keep going
through the night until dawn
on Friday and Saturday nights,
and nearly all charge for entry
(this usually includes a drink).
For impromptu raves, theme
nights and house parties
outside Paris, with shuttles
provided, check *Pariscope*'s
English section or key in to
Minitel 3615 Party News.

81

Bars, Wine Bars & Cybercafés

BARS

SO MUCH CHOICE

Paris has a huge number of wonderful bars and wine bars to choose from. These range from bars selling just beer, to cocktail and late-night bars dotted throughout the city. Most Parisian wine bars are small, neighbourly places, some selling food as well. You will find a great selection of regional wines. Explore the various neigbourhoods to find a plethora of convivial drinking holes.

BAR DU MARCHÉ

Retro interior and terrace looking out onto a lively market street. A Parisian favourite.

✚ K8 ✉ 75 rue de Seine 75006 ☎ 01 43 26 55 15 ⏰ Daily 8am–2am Ⓜ Odéon

BAR HEMINGWAY

An elegant bar in the luxury Ritz hotel, where old malts, champagne and cigars are *de rigueur*.

✚ J4 ✉ Hôtel Ritz, place Vendôme ☎ 01 43 16 33 65 ⏰ Mon–Sat 6.30pm–2am Ⓜ Opéra, Madeleine

BARRAMUNDI

Draws a fashionable crowd with its world music, bar, lounge and restaurant with a wide global menu. The interior combines influences from India and Africa.

✚ K3 ✉ 3 rue Taitbout 75009 ☎ 01 47 70 21 21 ⏰ Mon–Fri noon–2.30pm, 7pm–2am, Sat 7pm–5am Ⓜ Richelieu-Drouot, Chaussée d'Antin

BIRDLAND

An old Saint-Germain favourite. Relaxed atmosphere, with great jazz records.

✚ K8 ✉ 20 rue Princesse 75006 ☎ 01 43 26 97 59 ⏰ Daily 7pm–6am (opens at 2.30pm on Sat) Ⓜ Mabillon

CAFÉ CHARBON

Trendy café-bar with a mirrored interior. Enjoy the budget snacks or read the papers here until 2am.

✚ Off map at Q4 ✉ 109 rue Oberkampf 75011 ☎ 01 43 57 55 13 ⏰ Daily 8am–2am Ⓜ Parmentier

CAFÉ MARTINI

A cosy café/bar with a beamed ceiling, deep carpets and jazz music.

✚ Off map at Q7 ✉ 11 rue du Pas-de-la-Mule 75004 ☎ 01 42 77 05 04 ⏰ Daily 8.30am–2am Ⓜ Chemin-Vert

CAFÉ NOIR

Late-night haunt on fringe of Les Halles. High-decibel rock and an unmistakable techni-colour exterior.

✚ M4/M5 ✉ 65 rue Montmartre 75002 ☎ 01 40 39 07 36 ⏰ Mon–Fri 8am–2am, Sat 2pm–2am Ⓜ Sentier

CHINA CLUB

A classy cocktail bar with a restaurant serving Chinese cuisine. Art deco meets colonial in the decor.

✚ Off map at Q8 ✉ 50 rue de Charenton 75012 ☎ 01 43 43 82 02 ⏰ Daily 7pm–2am Ⓜ Ledru Rollin, Bastille

LA FOURMI

A great bar with retro furnishings and funky bottle-rack chandelier for before or after concerts at one of the many surrounding music venues. Young hip crowd.

✚ Montmartre map ✉ 74 rue des Martyrs 75018 ☎ 01 42 64 70 35 ⏰ Mon–Thu 8am–2am, Fri, Sat 8am–4am Ⓜ Pigalle

LE FUMOIR

For cocktails and book-browsing (3,000-book library) near the Louvre. Smooth crowd with young professionals frequenting the modern-style restaurant.

✚ L6 ✉ 6 rue de l'Amiral-de-Coligny 75001 ☎ 01 42 92 00 24 ⏰ Daily 11am–2am Ⓜ Louvre-Rivoli

HARRY'S NEW YORK BAR

Popular with the British, this bar offers hundreds of cocktails, perfectly mastered by the highly professional bar staff.

✚ J4 ✉ 5 rue Daunou 75002 ☎ 01 42 61 71 14 🕐 Mon–Sat 11am–3am, Sun noon–3am Ⓜ Opéra

LE MOLOKO

Cavernous, popular venue with a lounge bar upstairs and a dance floor below.

✚ Montmartre map ✉ 26 rue Fontaine 75009 ☎ 01 48 74 50 26 🕐 Daily 11pm–7am Ⓜ Blanche

LA TARTINE

An old daytime classic. French wines by the glass, cold platters of charcuterie and cheese.

✚ P7 ✉ 24 rue de Rivoli 75004 ☎ 01 42 72 76 85 🕐 8am–midnight; closed Mon Ⓜ St-Paul

LE TRAIN BLEU

Striking belle-époque setting that functions as a restaurant-bar. The food is pricey; stick to drinks.

✚ Off map at Q8 ✉ 1st floor, Gare de Lyon 75012 ☎ 01 43 43 09 06 🕐 Mon–Fri 7.30am–11pm, Sat–Sun 9am–11pm Ⓜ Gare de Lyon

LES EDITEURS

'The editors' attracts a literary crowd, who enjoy the comfortable velvet armchairs and library.

✚ K8 ✉ 4 carrefour de l'Odéon 75006 ☎ 01 43 26 67 76 🕐 Daily 8am–2am Ⓜ Odéon

PIANO VACHE

A good place to listen to acoustic music while enjoying draught beer. Located in the Latin Quarter.

✚ M10 ✉ 8 rue Laplace 75005 ☎ 01 46 33 75 03 🕐 Mon–Fri noon–2am, Sat–Sun 9pm–2am Ⓜ Maubert-Mutualité

RÉSERVOIR

This bar, in the Bastille area, draws a trendy crowd with its luxurious yet funky interior and lively atmosphere.

✚ Off map at Q8 ✉ 16 rue de la Forge-Royale 75011 ☎ 01 43 56 39 60 🕐 Mon–Thu 8pm–2am, Fri, Sat, 8pm–4am, Sun noon–4am Ⓜ Ledru-Rollin

CYBERCAFÉS

ACCESS ACADEMY

Huge internet café with over 400 computers in the heart of Saint-Germain-des-Prés.

✚ L8 ✉ 60–62 rue Saint André-des-Arts 75006 ☎ 01 43 25 23 80 🕐 Daily 8am–2am Ⓜ Odéon, St-Michel

SPUTNIK

Hip futurist cybercafé and cocktails in the charming village of Butte aux Cailles. Although not exactly central, it's worth the trip.

✚ Off map at N11 ✉ 14 rue de la Butte aux Cailles 75013 ☎ 01 45 65 19 82 🕐 Mon–Sat 2pm–2am, Sun 4pm–midnight Ⓜ Corvisart or Place d'Italie

XS-ARENA

The largest of a chain of cybercafés in Paris with over 200 computers.

✚ M6 ✉ 43 boulevard de Sébastopol 75001 ☎ 01 40 13 02 60 🕐 Daily 24 hours Ⓜ Châlet

STEAMBATHS

If nocturnal bar-crawling becomes too much, why not sweat it out at a steambath? The hammam at La Mosquée (✉ 39 rue Geoffroy Saint-Hilaire 75005 ☎ 01 43 31 38 20 ➤ 54) offers a lovely tiled interior à la Marrakesh (🕐 Men: Tue 2pm–9pm, Sun 10am–9pm Women: Mon, Wed, Thu, Sat 10am–9pm, Fri 2pm–9pm). A new though pricier alternative is Les Bains du Marais (✉ 31 rue des Blancs-Manteaux 75004 ☎ 01 44 61 02 02; www.lesbainsdumarais.com 🕐 Men: Thu 11am–11pm, Fri, Sat 10am–8am. Women: Mon 11am–8pm, Tue 11am–11pm, Wed 10am–7pm. Mixed: Wed 7am–11pm, Sat 10am–8pm, Sun 11am–11pm).

Theatres & Special Cinemas

CINEPHILE'S PARADISE

French films are once again dominating the home market (approximately half of tickets bought in French cinemas are for French films). With some 350 films shown each day, the choice can be tantalizing. Foreign films shown in their original languages have '*VO*' (*version originale*) after the title. New films come out on Wednesdays, which is also the day for all-round reductions. The Gaumont, MK2 and UGC cinemas offer multiple-entry cards that can be used for up to three people and save precious euros.

BOUFFES DU NORD

Many plays staged by director Peter Brook are not only excellent but also in English.

✚ Montmartre map ✉ 37 boulevard de la Chapelle 75010 ☎ 01 46 07 34 50; www.bouffes dunord.com ⊜ La Chapelle

CAFÉ D'EDGAR

This café-theatre is a springboard for new comedy talent.

✚ Off map at H11 ✉ 58 boulevard Edgar Quinet 75014 ☎ 01 42 79 97 97 ⊜ Edgar Quinet

LA CINÉMATHÈQUE FRANÇAISE

Cinema classics, with foreign films always in the original language.

✚ M3 ✉ 42 boulevard Bonne-Nouvelle 75010 (closed for 6 months from Mar 2005 during move to 51 rue de Bercy 75012; www.cinematheque francaise.co, ☎ 01 56 26 01 01 ⊜ Bonne-Nouvelle

COMÉDIE FRANÇAISE

This theatre, established in 1680, is home to France's most prestigious troupe of actors, originally formed by Molière. Performances of great classics, including Shakespeare and Molière.

✚ K5 ✉ 2 rue de Richlieu ☎ 01 44 58 15 15 www.comedie-francaise.fr ⊜ Palais Royal

L'ENTREPOT

Stimulating programme of art films and cult movies from all over the world, show in their original language. Bar-restaurant.

✚ Off map at G11 ✉ 7–9 rue Francis-de-Pressensé 75014 ☎ 01 45 40 07 50 ⊜ Pernety

FORUM DES IMAGES

Films or documentaries shot in or connected with Paris, and film classics. A cheap day pass admits you to four different films.

✚ M6 ✉ Port Saint-Eustache, Forum des Halles, Porte Sainte-Eustache 75001 ☎ 01 44 76 62 00 ⊜ Les Halles

LA PAGODE

A unique film theatre housed inside an exotic oriental pagoda shows cult clssics and modern arty films. Adjoining tea room and garden.

✚ F8 ✉ 57 bis rue de Babylone 75007 ☎ 01 45 55 48 48 ⊜ St-François Xavier

STUDIO GALANDE

Eclectic programme of screenings, from recent art films to cartoons. Cult movie *The Rocky Horror Picture Show* is on every Friday and Saturday— come dressed up if you're feeling brave!

✚ M9 ✉ 42 rue Galande 75005 ☎ 01 43 26 94 08 ⊜ St-Michel

THÉÂTRE DE BOBIGNY/LA MAISON DE LA CULTURE

A bit far out but worth the detour to be rewarded with some innovative avant-garde productions.

✚ Off map ✉ 1 boulevard Lénine, Bobigny ☎ 01 41 60 72 72; www.mc93.com ⊜ Bobigny-Pablo Picasso

THÉÂTRE DE NESLE

Small Left Bank theatre in the vaulted basement of a 17th-century mansion. English-language plays; also puppet shows for kids.

✚ L8 ✉ 8 rue de Nesle 75006 ☎ 01 46 34 61 04 ⊜ Odéon

Sport

AQUABOULEVARD

Huge family complex with water-shoots, palm trees, Jacuzzis. Gym, putting greens, tennis and squash courts too—at a price.

➕ Off map at A11 ✉ 4–6 rue Louis Armand 75015 ☎ 01 40 60 10 00 🚇 Balard

CLUB QUARTIER LATIN

This fitness complex offers an aquagym, cardio training, squash courts and a sauna. The club gets busy at peak times.

➕ N9 ✉ 19 rue de Pontoise 75005 ☎ 01 55 42 77 88 🚇 Maubert-Mutualité

HIPPODROME DE LONGCHAMP

Longchamp is where the hats and champagne come out for the annual Prix de l'Arc de Triomphe. Regular flat-races.

➕ Off map ✉ Bois de Boulogne 75016 ☎ 01 44 30 75 00 🚇 Porte d'Auteuil, then free bus

HIPPODROME DE VINCENNES

Colourful harness racing pulls in the crowds. The Prix d'Amérique is the top harness race of the season.

➕ Off map ✉ 2 route de la Ferme, Bois de Vincennes 75012 ☎ 01 49 77 17 17 🚇 Château de Vincennes, then shuttle

PARC DES PRINCES

Huge municipal stadium takes 50,000 spectators for major domestic football (soccer) and rugby games and home to Paris Saint-Germain FC. Home to the Musée National du Sport.

➕ Off map at A10 ✉ 24 rue du Commandant-Guilbaud 75016 ☎ 08 25 07 50 78 🚇 Porte d'Auteuil

PARIS VÉLO

Guided bicycle tours, in French and English, with titles such as Heart of Paris, Paris at Dawn and Unusual Paris. Reservations are required. Bicycle hire available.

➕ Off map at Q9 ✉ 22 rue Alphonse Baudin 75011 ☎ 01 48 87 60 01; www.parisvelosympa.com 🚇 Richard Lenoir

PISCINE DES HALLES (SUZANNE BERLIOUX)

Underground 50-m pool overlooked by lush tropical garden.

➕ M6 ✉ 10 place de la Rotonde 75001 ☎ 01 42 36 98 44 🚇 Les Halles

POPB

This Bercy venue hosts major sports events, as well as concerts. It can seat up to 17,000 people.

➕ Off map at Q10 ✉ 8 boulevard de Bercy 75012 ☎ 01 40 02 60 60 🚇 Bercy

STADE DE FRANCE

Built for the 1998 Football World Cup, this 60,000-seat stadium attained an almost mythical status following France's victory.

➕ Off map ✉ rue Francis-de-Pressensé 93210 Saint Denis ☎ 08 92 70 09 00; www.stadefrance.fr 🚉 RER, B: La Plaine—Stade de France 🚇 St-Denis, Porte de Paris

ROLAND-GARROS

Home to the eponymous tennis tournament, with 24 tennis courts and space for 39,000 spectators.

➕ Off map at A10 ✉ 2 avenue Gordon-Bennett 75016 ☎ 01 47 43 48 00; www.rolandgarros.org 🚇 Porte d'Auteuil, then walk

POOLS AND HORSES

Paris's municipal swimming pools have complicated opening hours that are largely geared to schoolchildren. Phone beforehand to check for public hours and avoid Wednesdays and Saturdays, both popular with children off school. If horse-racing is your passion, don't miss the harness racing at Vincennes with its brilliant flashes of colour-coordinated horses and jockeys. Check Paris-Turf for race programmes.

GET YOUR SKATES ON

In-line skating is popular in Paris and hundreds of people turn out to the Friday night tours organized by Pari Roller. Experienced skaters are welcome to join the three-hour ride, which starts from Montparnasse at 10pm (check details on www.pari-roller.com before setting out; check your insurance coverage). On Saturday afternoons the Rollers and Coquillages Society organizes a three-hour ride starting from Nomades sports shop, ✉ 37 boulevard Bourdon, Bastille ☎ 01 44 54 07 44; www.nomadeshop.com. 🕑 2.30pm.

Luxury Hotels

PRICES

Expect to pay over €350 for a double room in the luxury category.

LE CRILLON

Whether you stay at the Ritz, the Crillon, the Meurice, the Bristol or the Georges V, they all have their tales to tell, but that of the Crillon is perhaps the most momentous. This mansion managed to survive the Revolution despite having the guillotine on its doorstep. Mary Pickford and Douglas Fairbanks spent their honeymoon here.

HOTEL DE CRILLON

Fabulous Parisian classic that reeks glamour, style, history and major investments. 87 rooms plus 60 suites.

🔳 G4 ✉ 10 place de la Concorde 75008 (Concorde/Champs Élysées) ☎ 01 44 71 15 00; fax 01 44 71 15 02; www.crillon.com 🚇 Concorde

L'HÔTEL

A Parisian legend redolent of Oscar Wilde's last days. Piano-bar and restaurant, and some superb rooms. 16 rooms and 4 suites.

🔳 K7 ✉ 13 rue des Beaux Arts 75006 (Saint-Germain-des-Prés) ☎ 01 44 41 99 00; fax 01 43 25 64 81; www.l-hotel.com 🚇 St-Germain-des-Prés

HÔTEL DU JEU DE PAUME

A small, delightful hotel carved out of a 17th-century royal tennis court. 28 tasteful rooms with beams and marble bathrooms; some suites. No restaurant.

🔳 P8/P9 ✉ 54 rue Saint-Louis-en-l'Île 75004 (Île Saint-Louis) ☎ 01 43 26 14 18; fax 01 40 46 02 76; www.jeudepaumehotel.com 🚇 Pont Marie

HÔTEL MONTALEMBERT

A fashionable Left Bank hotel with a garden-patio, bar and restaurant. Chic design details and 56 well-appointed rooms. Popular with Americans.

🔳 H7 ✉ 3 rue de Montalembert 75007 (Saint-Germain-des-Prés) ☎ 01 45 49 68 68; fax 01 45 49 69 49; www.montalembert.com 🚇 Rue du Bac

HÔTEL SAINTE BEUVE

Exclusive establishment between the heart of Montparnasse and the Luxembourg gardens. Period antiques mix happily with modern furnishings. 22 rooms.

🔳 J11 ✉ 9 rue Sainte-Beuve 75006 (Montparnasse) ☎ 01 45 48 20 07; fax 01 45 48 67 52; www.paris-hotel-charme.com 🚇 Notre-Dame des Champs

HÔTEL SAN RÉGIS

Elaborately decorated hotel but modest in scale; popular with showbiz folk. Restaurant for hotel guests only. 44 rooms.

🔳 D5 ✉ 12 rue Jean-Goujon 75008 (Champs Élysées) ☎ 01 44 95 16 16; fax 01 45 61 05 48; www.hotel-sanregis.fr 🚇 Alma-Marceau

PAVILLON DE LA REINE

This hotel set back from place des Vosges, boasts a flowery courtyard and lovely leafy garden. Plenty of period decoration and lavish furnishings. No restaurant. 55 rooms.

🔳 Q7 ✉ 28 place des Vosges, 75003 (Marais) ☎ 01 40 29 19 19; fax 01 40 29 19 20; www.pavillon-de-la-reine.com 🚇 Bastille

LES RIVES DE NOTRE-DAME

This four-star hotel, overlooking the banks of the Seine, has beamed ceilings, marble tiling, colourful tapestries and fine wrought-iron furniture. 9 rooms and 1 suite.

🔳 M8 ✉ 15 quai St-Michel 75005 (Latin Quarter) ☎ 01 43 54 81 16; fax 01 43 26 27 09 www.rivesdenotredame.com 🚇 St-Michel

Mid-Range Hotels

HÔTEL DE L'ABBAYE SAINT-GERMAIN

This quaint, historic hotel was once a convent. The lounge and most of the 42 rooms look out onto a patio. Four suites have a private terrace. 37 rooms.

✚ J9 ✉ 10 rue Cassette 75006 (Saint-Sulpice) ☎ 01 45 44 38 11; fax 01 45 48 07 86; www.hotel-abbaye.com ⊕ St-Sulpice

ANGLETERRE SAINT-GERMAIN-DES-PRÉS

Former 18th-century British embassy. Garden patio, 27 spacious rooms where Hemingway once lived. Bar and piano lounge. No restaurant.

✚ J7 ✉ 44 rue Jacob 75006 (Saint-Germain-des-Prés) ☎ 01 42 60 34 72; fax 01 42 60 16 93; www.hotel-dngleterre.com ⊕ St-Germain-des-Prés

HÔTEL DUC DE SAINT-SIMON

Rather pricey but the antiques and picturesque setting just off boulevard Saint-Germain justify it. 34 comfortable rooms, intimate atmosphere. Reserve in advance.

✚ H7 ✉ 14 rue Saint-Simon 75007 (Saint-Germain-des-Prés) ☎ 01 44 39 20 20; fax 01 45 48 68 25; www.hotelducde saintsimon.com ⊕ Rue du Bac

HÔTEL LENOX

Popular with the design and fashion world. Chase T. S. Eliot's ghost and enjoy the restored, stylish 1930s bar. 34 rooms.

✚ J7 ✉ 9 rue de l'Université 75007 (Saint-Germain-des-Prés) ☎ 01 42 96 10 95; fax 01 42 61 52 83; www.lenoxsaintgermain.com ⊕ St-Germain-des-Prés

HÔTEL DES MARRONIERS

Oak-beamed rooms and vaulted cellars are converted to lounges. Ask for a room overlooking the garden. 37 rooms.

✚ K8 ✉ 21 rue Jacob 75006 (Saint-Germain-des-Prés) ☎ 01 43 25 30 60; fax 01 40 46 83 56; www.pairs-hotel-marronniers. com ⊕ St-Germain-des-Prés

HÔTEL MOLIÈRE

On a quiet street near the Louvre and Opéra. 32, clean, reasonably priced rooms. No restaurant.

✚ K5 ✉ 21 rue Molière 75001 (Opéra) ☎ 01 42 96 22 01; fax 01 42 60 48 68; www.hotel-moliere.fr ⊕ Pyramides, Palais-Royal

HÔTEL LA PERLE

Renovated 18th-century building on a quiet street near Saint-Germain. 38 rooms.

✚ J8 ✉ 14 rue des Canettes 75006 (Saint-Germain-de-Prés) ☎ 01 43 29 10 10; fax 01 46 34 51 04; www.hotellaperle.com ⊕ Mabillon

HÔTEL QUEEN MARY

Big bedrooms, an elegant lounge and small patio. 35 rooms and 1 suite

✚ H3 ✉ 9 rue Greffulhe 75008 (Opéra) ☎ 01 42 66 40 50; fax 01 42 66 94 92; www.hotelqueenmary.com ⊕ Madeleine, Havre-Caumartin

RÉSIDENCE LORD BYRON

Comfortable, classy 31-room hotel just off the Champs Élysées. Small garden.

✚ D2 ✉ 5 rue Châteaubriand 75008 (Champs Élysées) ☎ 01 43 59 89 98; fax 01 42 89 46 04 ⊕ George V

PRICES

A moderately priced hotel will charge €100–€300 for a double room.

THREE-STAR RATING

All these three-star establishments are obvious favourites with business travellers, so it is virtually impossible to find rooms during trade-fair seasons such as May to early June and mid-September to October. In summer many offer discounts as their clientele shrinks. All rooms are equipped with colour TV, direct-dial phone, private bath or shower rooms, minibar and most with hair dryer. Air-conditioning is not standard, but elevators are common.

APARTMENTS

For those staying longer than one night, renting an apartment makes good financial sense. The UK-based Apartment Service offers a wide selection of deluxe and standard apartments throughout central Paris (☎ +44 20 8944 1444; fax + 44 20 8944 6744; email: res@apartment.co.uk; Internet: www.apartment.co.uk). Also try Home Rental Service (✉ 120 avenue Champs Elysées ☎ 01 42 25 65 40; fax 01 42 25 65 45; www.homerental.fr) or Paris Lodging (☎ 01 43 36 71 69; fax 01 43 36 64 72; www.parislodging.fr).

Budget Accommodation

PRICES

You should be able to find a double room in a budget hotel for under €100.

BUDGET HOTELS

Gone are the heady days when Paris was peppered with atmospheric one-star hotels with their inimitable signs *'eau à tous les étages'* (water on every floor). Now there are bath or shower rooms with every bedroom, resulting in higher prices and smaller rooms. So don't expect much space in budget hotel rooms, but do expect breakfast and receptionists who speak a second language in every hotel with two or more stars.

BED-AND-BREAKFAST

For bed-and-breakfast, staying with host families, try Alcôve & Agapes–additional services include evening meal, French conversation, baby sitting (✉ 8 bis rue Coysevox 75018 ☎ 01 44 85 06 05; www.bed-and-breakfast-in-paris.com) or France Lodge (✉ 2 rue Meissonier 75017 ☎ 01 56 33 85 85; www.apartments-in-paris.com).

YOUTH HOSTELS

One way of seeing Paris on a budget is to stay in a youth hostel. Try the Auberge Internationale des Jeunes (✚ Off map at Q8 ✉ 10 rue Trousseau 75011 ☎ 01 47 00 62 00; fax 01 47 00 33 16; wwwaijparis.com), which offers shared rooms in the lively Bastille area at rock-bottom prices. Don't expect anything fancy, but the atmosphere is friendly. 200 rooms.

GRAND HÔTEL MALHER

Family hotel with 31 well-equipped rooms; excellent location.
✚ Q7 ✉ 5 rue Malher 75004 (Marais) ☎ 01 42 72 60 92; fax 01 42 72 25 37 Ⓜ St-Paul

HÔTEL DE L'AVRE

Minutes from the Eiffel Tower, an impeccably kept two-star hotel. Breakfast is served in the pretty garden in spring and summer. 26 rooms.
✚ Off map at C9 ✉ 21 rue de l'Avre 75015 (Champs de Mars) ☎ 01 45 75 31 03; fax 01 45 75 63 26; www.hoteldelavre.com Ⓜ La Motte-Picquet Grenelle

HÔTEL ANDRÉ GILL

Charming courtyard setting on quiet side street. 33 renovated rooms, reasonably priced.
✚ Montmartre map ✉ 4 rue André-Gill 75018 (Pigalle) ☎ 01 42 62 48 48; fax 01 42 62 77 92 Ⓜ Pigalle

HÔTEL DU COLLÈGE DE FRANCE

Tranquil 29-room hotel near the Sorbonne.
✚ M9 ✉ 7 rue Thénard 75005 (Quartier Latin) ☎ 01 43 26 78 36; fax 01 46 34 58 29; www.hotel-collegedefrance.com Ⓜ Maubert-Mutualité

HÔTEL ESMERALDA

Popular dollhouse hotel near Notre Dame. 15 reasonably priced rooms.
✚ M8 ✉ 4 rue Saint-Julien-le-Pauvre 75005 (Quartier Latin) ☎ 01 43 54 19 20; fax 01 40 51 00 68 Ⓜ St-Michel

HÔTEL JARDIN DES PLANTES

Pretty hotel overlooking the botanical gardens.

Good facilities. 33 rooms.
✚ N11 ✉ 5 rue Linné 75005 (Quartier Latin) ☎ 01 47 07 06 20; fax 01 47 07 62 74; www.timhotel.com Ⓜ Jussieu

HÔTEL DE LA PLACE DES VOSGES

Charming 17th-century town house in a quiet street close to place des Vosges. Basic comforts; excellent location with some good views over the rooftops from some of the 16 rooms.
✚ Q8 ✉ 12 rue de Birague 75004 (Marais/Bastille) ☎ 01 42 72 60 46; fax 01 42 72 02 64 Ⓜ Bastille, St-Paul

HÔTEL RÉCAMIER

Tranquil, friendly little hotel close to Saint-Germain and the Luxembourg gardens. 30 rooms.
✚ J9 ✉ 3 bis place Saint-Sulpice 75006 (Saint-Germain-des-Prés) ☎ 01 43 26 04 89; 01 46 33 27 73 Ⓜ St-Sulpice

HÔTEL SAINT-HONORÉ

A one-star hotel on the chic rue St-Honoré. Pristin decor in the 29 rooms.
✚ L6 ✉ 85 rue St-Honoré 75001 (Les Halles) ☎ 01 42 36 20 38; fax 01 42 21 44 08; www.hotelsainthonore.com Ⓜ Louvre-Rivoli, Châtelet

HÔTEL DE LA SORBONNE

On a quiet side street near the Sorbonne. 37 small but comfortable rooms. Well established and unpretentious.
✚ L10 ✉ 6 rue Victor-Cousin 75005 ☎ 01 43 54 58 08; fax 01 40 51 05 18; www.hotelsorbonne.com Ⓜ Cluny-La Sorbonne

PARIS
travel facts

AVENUE
DES
CHAMPS ÉLYSÉES

ESSENTIAL FACTS

Credit cards
- Credit cards are widely accepted.
- VISA cards (including MasterCard and Diners Club) can be used in cash dispensers. Most machines flash up instructions in the language you choose.
- American Express is less common, so Amex cardholders needing cash should use American Express ✉ 11 rue Scribe 75009 ☎ 01 47 77 70 00 🚇 Opéra

Electricity
- Voltage is 220V and sockets take two round pins.

Etiquette
- Shake hands on introduction and on leaving; once you know people better replace this with a peck on both cheeks.
- Always use *vous* unless the other person breaks into *tu*.
- It is polite to add *Monsieur*, *Madame* or *Mademoiselle* when addressing strangers or salespeople.
- Always say *bonjour* and *au revoir* in shops.
- When calling waiters, use *Monsieur* or *Madame* (not *garçon*).
- Dress carefully. More emphasis is put on grooming in France than in other countries.

Foreign exchange
- Only banks with *change* signs change foreign currency/traveller's cheques; a passport is necessary. Bureax de change are open longer hours but rates can be poorer. Rates for cashing euro traveller's cheques can be high.
- Airport and station exchange desks are open daily between 6.30am and 11pm.

Lavatories
- Public lavatory booths are common, and are generally well maintained.
- Every café has a lavatory ('Les toilettes, s'il vous plaît?') although standards vary, but you should order a drink first.

National holidays
- 1 January, Easter Monday, 1 May, 8 May, Ascension (a Thursday in May), Whit Monday (late May or early June), 14 July, 15 August, 1 November, 11 November, 25 December.
- Sunday services for public transport operate; many local shops, restaurants and even large stores disregard national holidays.

Opening hours
- Banks: Mon–Fri 9–noon, 2–4. Closed on public holidays and often the preceding afternoon.
- Post offices: Mon–Fri 8–7, Sat 8–noon. The central post office (✉ 52 rue du Louvre 75001) provides a 24-hour service for post, telegrams and telephone.
- Shops: Mon–Sat 9–7 or 10–8. Some close Monday and an hour at lunch. Many close during August. Arab-owned groceries stay open until 9 or 10pm daily.
- Museums: national museums close on Tuesday, municipal museums on Monday. Individual opening hours vary considerably; always phone to check hours for national holidays.

Places of worship
- Protestant churches: American Church ✉ 65 quai d'Orsay 75007 ☎ 01 40 62 05 00 🚇 Invalides
- St George's English Church ✉ 7 rue Auguste Vacquerie 75016 ☎ 01 47 20 22 51 🚇 Charles de Gaulle-Étoile, Kleber

- Jewish: Synagogue ✉ 10 rue Pavée 75004 ☎ 01 48 87 21 54 Ⓜ St-Paul
- Russian Orthodox: Saint Alexandre Nievski ✉ 12 rue Daru 75008 ☎ 01 42 27 37 34 Ⓜ Courcelles, Ternes

Student travellers

- An International Student Identity Card can reduce cinema charges, entrance to museums and air and rail travel.
- MIJE (Maison Internationale de la Jeunesse et des Étudiants) ✉ 6 rue de Fourcy 75004 ☎ 01 42 74 23 45 Ⓜ St-Paul Ⓞ Daily 7am–1am. Gives advice on hostel accommodation, and discounts on train tickets.
- CIDJ (Centre d'Information et de Documentation Jeunesse) ✉ 101 quai Branly 75015 ☎ 01 44 49 12 00 Ⓜ Bir-Hakeim Ⓞ Mon, Wed, Fri 10–6, Tue, Thu 10–7, Sat 9.30–1). Youth information centre for jobs, courses, sport.

Tourist Information Office

- Office du Tourisme de Paris ✉ 25 rue des Pyramides 75001 ☎ 08 92 68 30 00 Ⓞ Jun–end Oct daily 9–7; Nov–end May 10–7 (Sun from 11) Ⓜ Pyramides English-speaking staff.

PUBLIC TRANSPORT

Métro

- Métro lines are identified by their final destination and a number; connections are indicated with orange panels marked *correspondances* on the platform.
- Blue *sortie* signs show the exits.
- The first Métros run at 5.30am, and the last around 12.30am.
- Keep your ticket until you exit— it has to be re-slotted on the RER, and ticket inspectors prowl the Métro.
- Try to avoid rush hours: 8–9.30am and 4.30–7pm.

Tickets and passes

- Tickets and passes function for Métro, buses and RER.
- One ticket givess access to the whole Métro network, the RER within Paris, Parisian and suburban buses. A *carnet* of ten tickets is considerably cheaper than individual tickets.
- Pass and suburban RER ticket prices depend on how many travel zones you intend to pass through.
- *Mobilis* is a one-day pass, valid on Métro, buses and RER.
- A *Paris Visite* card gives unlimited travel for one, two, three or five days plus discounts at certain monuments but you need to do a lot of travelling to make it pay.
- The Carte Orange pass (photo required) works with a *coupon hebdomadaire* (valid from Mon–Sun) or a *coupon mensuel* (valid for one calendar month).

MEDIA & COMMUNICATIONS

Post offices

- Stamps can be bought at *tabacs;* post mail in any yellow mailbox.
- All post offices have free access to the Minitel directory service, express courier post (Chronopost), phone booths and photocopying machines.

Press

- Main dailies are *Le Monde* (serious centre-left), *Libération* (left-wing) and *Le Figaro* (right-wing).
- Weekly news magazines range from the left-wing *Le Nouvel Observateur*, *L'Express* (centre) and *Le Point* (centre-right) to *Paris Match* and *Canard Enchaîné*. For weekly listings of cultural events (films, plays exhibitions), buy a copy of *L'Officiel des Spectacles*.

- Central newspaper kiosks and newsagents stock European dailies and *USA Today*; these are widely available on the day of issue.
- The NMPP's central bookshop (✉ 93 rue Montmartre 75002) has a range of French and foreign press, while the newsagents in the Carrousel beneath the Louvre carries American press and international fashion publications.

Telephones

- Most Parisian phone booths use France Telecom phone cards (*télécarte* for 50 or 120 units), available from post offices, *tabacs*, stations or at main Métro stations. A few booths still use coins, particularly those in cafés.
- Cheap periods for international calls vary: for Europe, Australia and New Zealand Mon–Sat 9.30pm–8am and all day Sun; for the USA and Canada, daily 2am–noon, with lesser reductions 8pm–2am.
- Information ☎ 12
- International information ☎ 3212
- To call France from the UK dial 00 33, then omit the first zero from the number. To call the UK from France, dial 00 44, then omit the first zero.
- International call via the operator ☎ 08 36 59 31 23
- To call France from the US dial 011 33, then leave out the first zero. To call the US from France dial 00 1.
- All French telephone numbers have ten digits.
- All numbers in the Île-de-France, including Paris, start with 01 unless at extra rates, when they start with 08, some are toll-free.
- To call the French provinces, use: 02 Northwest, 03 Northeast, 04 Southeast, 05 Southwest.

EMERGENCIES

Emergency phone numbers

- Crisis-line in English: SOS Help ☎ 01 46 21 46 46 🕐 3–11pm
- Police ☎ 17; European emergency ☎ 112
- Ambulance (SAMU) ☎ 15
- Fire (*sapeurs pompiers*) ☎ 18
- Anti-poison ☎ 01 40 05 48 48

Embassies and consulates

- British Embassy ✉ 35 rue du Faubourg-Saint-Honoré 75008 ☎ 01 44 51 31 00 🚇 Concorde
- British Consulate ✉ 16 rue d'Anjou 75008 ☎ 01 44 51 31 01/2 🚇 Concorde
- US Embassy ✉ 2 avenue Gabriel 75008 ☎ 01 43 12 22 22 🚇 Concorde
- US Consulate ✉ 2 rue Saint-Florentin 75001 ☎ 01 43 12 22 22
- Canadian Embassy ✉ 35 avenue Montaigne 75008 ☎ 01 44 43 29 00
- Canadian Consulate ✉ 35 avenue Montaigne 75008 ☎ 01 44 43 29 00 🚇 Franklin D. Roosevelt
- Australian Embassy ✉ 4 rue Jean-Rey 75015 ☎ 01 40 59 33 00 🚇 Bir-Hakeim
- New Zealand Embassy ✉ 7ter rue Léonard-de-Vinci 75016 ☎ 01 45 01 43 43 🚇 Victor Hugo

Lost property

- The police lost property office is ✉ 36 rue des Morillons 75015 ☎ 08 21 00 25 25 🕐 9–5 🚇 Convention

Medicines and medical treatment

- Minor ailments can often be treated at pharmacies (identified by a green cross), where staff will also advise on where to contact local doctors.
- All public hospitals have a 24-hour emergency service (*urgences*) as well as specialist doctors. Payment is made on the spot, but if you are hospitalized

ask to see the *assistante sociale* to arrange payment directly through your insurance.

- House calls are made with SOS Médecins ☎ 01 47 07 77 77, or for dental problems SOS Dentaire ☎ 01 43 37 51 00
- 24-hour pharmacy: Les Champs ✉ 84 avenue des Champs-Élysées 75008 ☎ 01 45 62 02 41
- The Drugstore chain at Champs Élysées offers pharmacies, newsagents, cafés and tobacconists open until 1.30am.

Precautions

- Watch wallets and handbags as pickpockets are active, particularly in crowded bars, flea markets, cinemas, railway stations and the airport.
- Keep traveller's-cheque numbers separate from the cheques.
- It is important to make a declaration at a local *commissariat* (police station) to claim losses on your insurance.
- Women are generally safe to travel alone or together, although the same risks apply as in any city in western Europe. Deal with any unwanted attention firmly and politely. Avoid the Métro at night.

LANGUAGE

Basic vocabulary
yes/no oui/ non
please s'il vous plaît
thank you merci
excuse me excusez-moi
hello bonjour
good evening bonsoir
goodbye au revoir
do you speak English? parlez-vous anglais?
I don't understand je ne comprends pas

how much? combien?
where is/are…? où est/sont…?
here/there ici/là
turn left/right tournez à gauche/droite
straight on tout droit
when? quand?
today aujourd'hui
yesterday hier
tomorrow demain
how long? combien de temps?
at what time? à quelle heure?
what time do you open/close? à quelle heure ouvrez/ fermez-vous?
do you have…? avez-vous…?
a single room une chambre simple
a double room une chambre double
with/without bathroom avec/sans salle de bains
breakfast le petit déjeuner
lunch le déjeuner
dinner le dîner
how much is this? c'est combien?
do you take credit cards? acceptez-vous des cartes de credit?
I need a doctor/dentist j'ai besoin d'un médecin/dentiste
can you help me? pouvez-vous m'aider?
where is the hospital? où est l'hôpital?
where is the police station? où est le commissariat?

1	un	16	seize
2	deux	17	dix-sept
3	trois	18	dix-huit
4	quatre	19	dix-neuf
5	cinq	20	vingt
6	six	21	vingt-et-un
7	sept	30	trente
8	huit	40	quarante
9	neuf	50	cinquante
10	dix	60	soixante
11	onze	70	soixante-dix
12	douze	80	quatre-vingts
13	treize	90	quatre-vingt-dix
14	quatorze	100	cent
15	quinze	1,000	mille

Index